HIDDEN TREASURES

OXFORDSHIRE

Edited by Claire Tupholme

First published in Great Britain in 2002 by
YOUNG WRITERS
Remus House,
Coltsfoot Drive,
Peterborough, PE2 9JX
Telephone (01733) 890066

All Rights Reserved

Copyright Contributors 2002

HB ISBN 0 75434 008 2
SB ISBN 0 75434 009 0

FOREWORD

This year, the Young Writers' Hidden Treasures competition proudly presents a showcase of the best poetic talent from over 72,000 up-and-coming writers nationwide.

Young Writers was established in 1991 and we are still successful, even in today's technologically-led world, in promoting and encouraging the reading and writing of poetry.

The thought, effort, imagination and hard work put into each poem impressed us all, and once again, the task of selecting poems was a difficult one, but nevertheless, an enjoyable experience.

We hope you are as pleased as we are with the final selection and that you and your family continue to be entertained with *Hidden Treasures Oxfordshire* for many years to come.

Contents

Molly Schofield	1
Sam Burnett	1
Beckley CE Primary School	
Hermionie Stanley	2
Maria Ridge	2
Harley Chalmers	3
Bledington Primary School	
Christopher Jennings	4
Nicholas Mark Hyatt	4
Martha Carrick	5
Emily Coombes	5
Jessica Rutherford	6
Sarah Ferryman	6
Liam Jarvis	7
Emily Milhench	7
Ben Truman	8
Rosanna Pearson	8
Callum Rose	8
Madeleine Milhench	9
Alexandra Elmer Ménage	9
Nick Pocock	10
Lucy Richardson	10
Stephanie Coles	10
Ducklington CE Primary School	
Rachel Dennis & Holly Lawrence	11
Charlotte Wood	11
Nichola Lee	11
Declan Burden	12
Hayley Rolls	12
Sarah Trinder	12
Sian Towns	13
Nicholas Grunwald	13

Charlie Emma Askew & Abbie Horne	13
Daniel Luffman	14
Emma-Jo Larney	14
Amy Snell	14
Emily Drake	15
Kimberley Smith	15
Jennifer Mills	15
David Gordon-Smith	16
Joshua Rimington	16
Stuart Weston	16
Lauren Titera & Jessie-May Edmonds	17
Craig Tredwell	17
Sam Hatton	18

Ewelme CE Primary School

Harry Barlow	18
Jordan Goldspink	18
Elspeth Walker	19
Kia Little	20
Gemma Bolton	21
Elliott Sean Hughes	22
Jonathan Lansley	22
Jordan Watts	23
Faron Watts	23
Laura Griffin	24
Hayley Jameson	24
Elizabeth Spence	25
Charlotte Moore	26
Rose Parker	26
Bella Maine	27
Jack Eccles	27
Jessica Jewitt	28
Olivia Stoddart	28
David Granat	29
Trudy Jones	30
Fran Walker	30
Christopher Perkins	31
Connie Jacobs	32

Lucinda Kenrick	32
Chloe Maine	33
Daniel Clements	34
Jessica Griffin	35
Rosie Duffield	36
Hannah Fitzgerald	36
Jessica Veitch	37
Charlie Walker	37
Ellie Clements	38
Rhys Thomas	39
Jack Ventress	40
Alex Butler	40
Elspeth Wilson	41
Kit Walker	41

Hanney CE Primary School

Lizzy Ewers	42
Grace Culley	42
Isobel Gahan	43
Robyn Dark	43
Andrew Hughes	44
Jack Tokelove	44
Emma Rebeckah Richens	44
Brett Sawyer	45
Lisa Little	45
Becky Aram	45
Edward Haynes	46
Imogen Stringfellow	46
Sarah Cornish	47
Christopher Sellwood	47
Lawrence Stringfellow	48
Adrian Pepler	48
Joe Griffiths	48
David Eltham	49

John Hampden Primary School

Robin Styles	49
Jonathan McIver	49

Emily Moore	50
Louise Gibbons	50
Hannah Beaugeard	51
Maisie Faulkner	51
Laura Dixon, Christopher Anderson, Mitchell Meredith & Maisie	52
Ina Coyle	52
Toby Maddox, Billy Wagerfield, Kirsty Clarke & Justyn Reed	53
Stephen Price	53
Adam Clark	54
Kirsty Smith	54
Zoë Francis	55
Nicole Blanco	55
Lisa Thomas	56
Lucy Hearn	56
Abi Mansfield	57
Daniel Hamp	57
Robert Rees	58
Thomas Merriman	58
Rebecca Hickling	58
Nick Palfrey	59
Anna Howarth	60
Wilber Sears	60
Dominic Stanway-Williams	61
Ben Lindsay	61
Vicky Plater	62
Helena Byrne-Stevens	63
Amanda Rawlings	63
George White	64
Laura Elliott	64
Luke Ounsworth	65
Ben Carrington	65
Elena Rees	66
Emily Braund	66
Annabel Grace	66
Ross McGoun	67
Jessica Evans	67

Sofie Jones	68
Isabella Whiteman	69

Millbrook CP School

Daniel Ferguson	69
Thomas Smith	70
Declan Laycock	70
Daniel Pope	71
George Jackson	72
Ashley Ward	72
Hayley Chapman	73
Liam Smith	74
Joe Braham	74
Jamie Burton	74
Jessica Peart	75
Jennifer Douch	75
Emily Steven-Fountain	75
Katie Evans	76
Katie-May Boulter	76
Georgina Naish	77
Luke Dady	78
Lewis Goulding	79
Samantha Boardman	79
Tom Bennett	80
James Lloyd	80
Sheridan Hetherington	80
Adam Badger	81
Hal Davison	81
Lewis King	81
Christina Wilkinson	82
April Haynes	82
Declan Dorsett	82
Sean Finegan	83
Barney Gill	83
Jodi Wallbridge-Marshall	83
Tommy Courtney	84
Martyn Lucas	84
Naomi Swinney	84

Shelley Syme	85
Lewis Butler	85
Jamie Hickman	86

New College School

Henry Anderson Elliott	86
James Millard	87
Clym Buxton	88
Charlie Littlewood	88
Andrew Crawford	89
Sam Clarke-Warry	90
Charlie Harnden	90
Wouter Vorstman	91
George Whittow	91
Alexis Kreager	92
Barnaby McCay	93
Otta Jones	94
Thomas Stell	94
Robert Brooks	95
Rhys Newcombe-Jones	96
Matthew Thorns	96

North Leigh CE Primary School

Natasha Dawe	97

Rupert House School

Katie Halfhead	97
Kate Swann	98
Celeste Moberly	98
Sophia Lerche-Thomsen	99
Katherine Innes	100
Annie Moberly	100
Hannah Baker	101
Ella Shepard	101
Camilla Hopkinson	102
Amira Burshan	102
Arabella Boardman	103
Laura Wheatley	103

Sophie McDowell	104
Rosie Thake	104
Victoria Bushnell	105
Alice Buys	106
Penny Hall	106
Olivia Barton	107
Alexandra Boardman	108
Alexandra Barbour	108
Lisa Szego	109
Amelia Thornton	109
Alicia Holder	110
Georgie Griffiths	110
Charly Binney	111
Tuula Costelloe	112
Georgina Williams-Gray	112
Emma Collinson	113
Katherine Poulter	114
Emily Granger	114
Ruth Collins	115
Emily Binning	116

St Laurence CE Primary School, Warborough

Adam Lubbock	116
Samantha Alfred	117
Richard Meadows	117
Callum McLarty	118
Jodie Stanley	119
Patrick Rider	120
Daniel Haynes	121
Sara Bailey	122
Emily Cox	123
Christopher Blevins	124
Bethan Curl	125
Rebecca Emerson	126
Mollie Hodge	127
Oliver Picken	128
Michael Gibbons	129

St Mary's School, Henley-On-Thames
- Harriet Kitching — 129
- Antonia Barker — 130
- Henry Svendsen — 130
- Charles Kronsten — 130
- Natalie Bishop — 131
- Elizabeth Walton — 131
- Fiona Stewart — 132
- Matthew Stewart — 132
- Guy Pawson — 133
- Ella May James — 133
- Hannah Nugent — 134
- Etienne Bataille — 134

Thomas Reade Primary School
- Robert Alderman — 135
- Nicholas Mould — 135
- Christopher Eccles — 136
- Katherine Hudson — 136
- Lucy White — 137
- Thomas Turner — 137
- Stephanie Gerring — 138
- Lucy Killoran & Sarah Woolhouse — 138
- Natalie O'Hare — 139
- Zoe Graubner — 139
- Rose Gallagher — 140
- Susan Shi — 140
- Matthew Wilson — 141
- Alastair Gregory — 141
- Naomi Keating — 142
- Hannah Burfitt — 143
- Dara Probets — 144
- Bridie Aldridge — 144
- Lisa Wood — 145
- Nicola North — 145
- Claire Liddiard & Sara Talman — 146
- Amber Parrott & Hannah Joyce — 147
- Robbie Hand — 148

Lucy Tyler	149
Mimi Kellard	150
Aaron Jane	150
Jonathan Mallion	151
Tom Hodson & Sanjay Sharma	152
Nishant Khataniar	152
Andrew Eccles	153

Tower Hill Primary School

Charlotte Whitlam & Kayleigh Estus	153
Luke Fry	154

Witney Community Primary School

Bethany Walker	154
Charlotte Hewson	155
Steve Barney	156
Amber Lee	156
Kirsty May Abberley	157
Melissa Gray	158
Sarah Dimond	158
Charlotte Rowe	159
Cheryl Birdseye	160
Shaun Killingbeck	160
Rebecca Jupp	161
Calum Hazell	162
Laura Dowsett	162
George Bone	163
Laura Hockey	164
Amy Skidmore	164
Laura Grant	165
Christopher James Barker	165
Ashley Ramsey	166
James Parry	167

Woodcote CP School

Emma Craig	167
Geoge Blower	168
Gemma Ford	168

Matthew Ploszynski	168
Leo Anderson	169
Connor Mattimore	169
Natasha Hyde	169
Genevieve Simpson	170
Jade Marshall	170
Anje Wessels	171

The Poems

ANGER MEETS LOVE

Anger is a bad man,
He eats the skin of dusty, dead people
And drinks their heart's blood!
He has fiery, red hair
And glittery, green eyes.
He has barbed wire eyelashes
And he wears scarlet and ebony.

One day he meets Love,
She has sapphire eyes and rosy lips.
She wears a dress of lilies
And she helps people who are injured in war.
Her skin is soft and pearly,
When Anger meets Love, he melts.

Molly Schofield (8)

AUTUMN

Autumn,
My favourite time of the year,
When brown crumpled leaves crunch under my feet
And autumn rain trickles down my back, giving me a tingle.
Our open fire providing me with warmth
From the cold and misty night.

Autumn,
The season of mist and mellow fruitfulness,
An early setting sun and more.
Where are the flowers for the bees
That thought that the warm days would never cease?
Where are the pretty birds
That sing the summer song?

Sam Burnett (10)

IN MY HEAD

In my head there is a world of animals,
Monkeys, elephants, penguins, flamingos.
I'm stroking tigers with soft fur,
Riding elephants with long trunks.

In my head there is a sailing world,
Me winning a gold medal,
Everyone cheering.
Singing the National Anthem,
British flag goes up.

In my head I am climbing trees,
Picking fruit,
Cocoa beans, bananas, coconuts, mangos,
Building tree houses.
Planting flowers for a garden,
Catching fish with braces and shoelaces,
Then, sleepyhead, I fall asleep.

Hermionie Stanley (9)
Beckley CE Primary School

THE RAINFOREST

A rainforest is full of enchantment,
The rivers and lakes flow calmly with a little sweep of wind,
All the flowers are full of light and it brings you into a tropical country,
Full of glory and gentleness.
Its powerful colour of green, but not all the same colour,
Different interesting shades of green,
The tall, strong, old and young trees full of creatures,
Taking you into their world.
Showing you the path to the most spectacular place you've ever seen,
Opening the secret door where it takes you into *boggy*
And slimy, squidgy mud holes.
Deeper down into the heart of the rainforest and through
An even more treasured door and out to freedom of lush
Paradise with waterfalls falling soothingly down,
Your neck, soaking into your skin.

Maria Ridge (10)
Beckley CE Primary School

A Memory

I'll tell you, shall I
Something I remember?
Something that still means
A great deal to me.
It was a long time ago,
It was very sad,
My granny called,
She said my grandad,
My wonderful, fit grandad,
Kept being sick,
He couldn't speak.
I remember she told me,
She rushed him to the hospital.
We went to see him in his room,
I remember him saying,
'I have cancer.'
He had lost his hair,
He was pale.
We, my dad and I, went to the cafeteria,
I bought him a bean toy,
Then we found out that he had died.
My mum, Hamish and I went home on the train,
I cried for a long time,
So did my mum.
I miss my grandad,
I've still got the toy,
I love him,
I just want him back.

Harley Chalmers (9)
Beckley CE Primary School

UNDER THE STAIRCASE

Under the staircase is a hidden cave
Where there was a hidden slave.
The hidden slave directed us to gold
As he was telling us we had to be bold.

The first thing I saw was a hidden chest
And inside was the very best
In the chest were pieces of gold
That nobody had ever got to hold

Under that were stacks of crystal
That had first been seen by a man with a pistol
I didn't bother about the locket
So I just threw most of them in my pocket

After that I made a dash
I went so fast you could see a flash
By accident I ran into the slave
But luckily I still got out of the cave.

Christopher Jennings (10)
Bledington Primary School

HIDDEN TREASURE

In the gloomy, dark house
There was an old, bare bookcase, behind it a box,
Golden, gleaming in the secret room. What might it be?
A pair of golden socks or golden crown jewels?
It might be money!
Then I'll be rich, I'll open it and see.
It's money! I'm rich,
Rich, hooray!

Nicholas Mark Hyatt (9)
Bledington Primary School

MUFFIN

I'm stuck in a cage,
I can't rage,
I scream and shout and jump about,
Here I am,
I can't get out.

I've got a house,
A wheel and a mouse,
Please tell me what I am,
I am . . .
Please tell me what I am.

All day and night,
I'm on the run,
Round and round and on my tum,
Please tell me what I am,
I am . . .
Please tell me what I am.

Martha Carrick (11)
Bledington Primary School

MATERIALS

M arble is hard and round
A luminium is a silvery colour
T iles are any colour
E lastic is strong and stretchy
R ubber can be grippy
I nk is lots of colours
A sh trees have a silver-grey bark
L eather is very thick
S oap is clean and slippery.

Emily Coombes (7)
Bledington Primary School

THE LOST TREASURE

Whales whistle,
Seagulls settle on the sea,
Seals and their pups dive,
Then slowly submerge.
The sea is full of life,
Then a terrifying noise.
A dark shape moves over,
Then a permanent black liquid.
The whales no longer whistle,
The seagulls no longer settle on the sea,
The seals and their pups no longer dive,
Then slowly submerge,
The sea is no longer full of life,
It's quiet and still,
But if you go out in a small boat,
You may find the lost treasure of the sea.

Jessica Rutherford (10)
Bledington Primary School

BEYOND THE SUNSET

Beyond the beautiful sunset of the summer,
I wonder what lies,
Were there's lots of amazing creatures
And wonderful features?
I looked around
And I frowned,
For there was a door
And beyond that was a beautiful sandy shore,
With gorgeous white horses,
Splashing their hooves in the waves.

Sarah Ferryman (11)
Bledington Primary School

DEATH TRAP DUNGEON

You don't want to go to Death Trap Dungeon,
It is all dark, cold and grim,
Only God knows what's down there,
In a fight you would not win!

Along the corridor and up the stairs,
Is where the zombie-dog lies,
First the dog will stare at you,
Then out pop his eyes.

The stench of an ogre's armpits
Is enough to make you cry,
If the Grim Reaper catches you,
Then prepare to *die*.

Liam Jarvis (10)
Bledington Primary School

UNDER THE OCEAN

On the ocean bed lie the plants
In sea so deep
Let the creatures sleep
While the whale snores
The dark chest creaks its doors
The ocean bed lies still
Not a word to be heard
Until the blue whale comes swimming over
Better stand on the other side
Otherwise you will take a trip inside
The morning wakes again.

Emily Milhench (9)
Bledington Primary School

The Hidden Sun

I was in an aeroplane,
Floating high above people,
High over everywhere,
Then suddenly I saw something glistening,
Yellow, orange and red mixed together,
It was hidden behind a cloud,
I looked, I saw something round burning,
Red-hot and coming towards us,
I was the first one to find the . . .
Hidden sun.

Ben Truman (8)
Bledington Primary School

Hidden Staircase

What's up the staircase? Nobody knows,
The rickety rackety staircase that could lead to gold,
I hope there's not a goblin with a wart on its nose
Or a witch that casts spells
And can turn you into toads.
The staircase is old and creaky,
It creaks when you walk up it
And I would love to find out what's up the
Rickety rackety staircase.

Rosanna Pearson (10)
Bledington Primary School

Does Anyone Care?

A scientist was very keen
To make his strange submarine,
He went down, down very deep,
To take the treasure for his keep.

The scientist never returned,
Some say he drowned or even burned.
The treasure's down there somewhere,
I wonder if anyone cares?

Callum Rose (10)
Bledington Primary School

BEYOND THE CLOUDS

Beyond the clouds it's all magic,
Nothing happens that's ever so tragic,
There's flying dolphins,
Swooping butterflies,
A golden, sparkling castle,
A funny rainbow-colour sky,
Unicorns leap,
Talking flowers,
Trees that walk,
Now you have been beyond the clouds,
To the land of magic way, way above.

Madeleine Milhench (9)
Bledington Primary School

UNDER THE SEA

Under the sea
It is just me!
I had one friend
At the end
Then she left me
The other dolphin's gone
Into a net
And now I am so sad.

Alexandra Elmer Ménage (9)
Bledington Primary School

DUNGEON

In the dungeon where nobody goes
There is a dragon without any clothes
Here comes a cowboy, clippety clop
Gets his phone and calls the cops

Here come the cops, clippety clop
Got their guns and shot the rock
They missed the dragon but hit the rock
Clippety clop, clippety clop.

Nick Pocock (10)
Bledington Primary School

I WONDER ...

I wonder where the end of the world is?
I wonder who sits in the street turning lights on and off?
I wonder what fairies lie above the clouds?
I wonder when the witches come out at night?
I wonder why nobody is allowed to see any of these people?
I wonder ...

Lucy Richardson (11)
Bledington Primary School

UNDER THE SEA

Under the sea live lots of creatures,
Each creature has lots of features,
They play, they fight,
It's not a pleasant sight,
When all the creatures are merry,
They celebrate with a glass of sherry.

Stephanie Coles (11)
Bledington Primary School

CHRISTMAS

The tree lights blink while the branches stretch out across the room,
The angel giggles in the bright light,
While the colourful baubles swing from side to side.
The snowman stares longingly into the warm, cackling fire
But doesn't notice the midday bell cry out *ding-dong*.
The mouth-watering food walks to the table jumping onto the
Shimmering china plates whilst the bubbling champagne
                                                gurgles impatiently.

Rachel Dennis (10) & Holly Lawrence (11)
Ducklington CE Primary School

NIGHT-TIME

The star winked at the people back on Earth.
The moon smiled at the world passing by.
The dark, still night was crying all alone.
The trees waved in the heavy wind.
The dark wind talked as it passed through the door
And the house pulled itself together.

Charlotte Wood (10)
Ducklington CE Primary School

THE CHRISTMAS TREE

The sparkling star daydreaming on the tree
With branches like arms.
The glowing lights chase each other
Round the green limbs.
The tickling tinsel reflects on the tree.
The swinging baubles dance on the tree.

Nichola Lee (10)
Ducklington CE Primary School

TORNADO

The tornado comes out of nowhere
Dancing round and round, it destroys every house
It whistles everywhere it goes
Snatching every roof and car
Less mercy than a soldier with a gun!
It spins and disappears into the deep fog.

Declan Burden (10)
Ducklington CE Primary School

SNOW

Twinkle, twinkle as they fall onto the ground,
As the leaves are bedded into the snow,
The coldness rises into the gutter,
As it crunches under the tree's feet,
It falls onto the branches of trees
And it crashes as it hits the kerb.

Hayley Rolls (11)
Ducklington CE Primary School

BIRTHDAY

A candle on a cake dances while we sing,
The paper wrestles when we open it,
Balloons bouncing round the room
While a gust of excitement rushes by
The room full of joy
While bags were handed out.

Sarah Trinder (11)
Ducklington CE Primary School

XMAS

The angel sitting on the top of the Christmas tree is singing
The lights on the tree are sparkling and winking
The fire is burning and spitting
The food in the oven is making the snowman want to come in and eat
The presents under the Christmas tree are gleaming
The cat is sitting on the mat with wide eyes
Getting ready to pounce.

Sian Towns (11)
Ducklington CE Primary School

WEATHER

The cloud fell lower and lower,
Over the climbing city the wind begins to howl,
The hail grinned as it punched humans in the face,
The fog laughed as it stopped people going out,
The rain jumped as it hit cars,
The sun's arms stretched out to clear it all away.

Nicholas Grunwald (10)
Ducklington CE Primary School

CHRISTMAS

The Christmas tree blushes as it stands proud in the corner,
With coloured baubles glistening in the flash of Christmas lights,
The twinkle of tinsel wrapped round the spiky green arms of the tree,
Outside in the freezing cold, the pond stands as still as ice,
The tall trees sway in the whistling wind,
Whilst the grass snuggles into a bed of snow.

Charlie Emma Askew (10) & Abbie Horne (11)
Ducklington CE Primary School

A Volcano

The volcano spits lava out of its mouth,
Whilst spreading over the ground like it's fell over.
The smouldering rocks have run out of air,
As they hit the ground.
The volcano coughs its last breath
And then stops flowing with lava.
The black cloud now walking away
As it calms down,
Now the sun smiles again over the Earth.

Daniel Luffman (11)
Ducklington CE Primary School

Xmas

The angel at the top of the tree is singing
The lights on the tree are sparkling and winking
The fire is burning and spitting
The food in the oven is making the snowman want to come in and eat it
The presents under the Christmas tree are gleaming with glee
The cat sitting on the mat with wide eyes, getting ready to pounce.

Emma-Jo Larney (10)
Ducklington CE Primary School

Birthdays

The candles on the cake dance
While we sing the paper wrestles when we open it
Balloons bounce round the hall while a gush of wind rushes by
The room's full of joy while the bags are given out.

Amy Snell (11)
Ducklington CE Primary School

CHRISTMAS POEM

Christmas presents unwrapping,
Babies clapping,
Wind blowing,
The night sky glowing,
The angels glowing and singing,
As the church bells are ringing,
Trees awaken,
Softly stretching by a bubbling lake,
Fire burning, lighting up the chimney,
Birds sleeping like the old neighbours.

Emily Drake (10)
Ducklington CE Primary School

NIGHT-TIME

The stars twinkle as they walked through the black sky.
The moon smiled at the splashing water gladly.
The darkness wraps round the Earth keeping everything warm.
The owls squeaking with the chimneys whistling.
The bouncing clouds are bringing stars closer.
The lampposts follow the cars down the road.

Kimberley Smith (11)
Ducklington CE Primary School

THE CHRISTMAS TREE

The sparkling star daydreaming on the tree with branches like arms
The glowing lights chase each other round the green limbs
The tickling tinsel reflects on the tree
The swinging baubles dance on the tree.

Jennifer Mills (10)
Ducklington CE Primary School

VOLCANO

The lava tumbling down the side of the volcano
Whilst the Earth shakes and the rocks jump out of the top
Then hit the floor with a thump
Animals scatter around
Mice trying to escape the running lava
Flowing like a river, it cleans the area of life
All that's left is a naked tree.

David Gordon-Smith (10)
Ducklington CE Primary School

THE FOG WAS CLEARED

The fog was cleared
Like a curtain being opened with unseen hands
The sun beamed down on Earth
Like a burning furnace
Then suddenly the lights went out
An eclipse, everlasting eclipse
The moon cleverly closed its eyelids on the sun.

Joshua Rimington (10)
Ducklington CE Primary School

A VOLCANO

The flickering, furious, fiery volcano blows its pipe
The rocks go flying and the volcano weeps out lava
The hot ash races the lava down
The sun fades as the mist snatches the light
Slowly and steadily the lava slows its walk
And the light starts to take back what's his.

Stuart Weston (11)
Ducklington CE Primary School

SNOW DANCE

Mother Nature's icy white tears start to drop
She draws out her black cloak

As the snow tears fall to the ground
They start to stand up and dance all around

Snow's tear bands starts to march
Hitting their drums and playing their sweet harp

The snowflake starts skipping down the black cloak
The tension rises as the drums get faster

She begins to dance to the harp in her dazzling silky dress
As the drums slow down she is looking her best

Alas the sun begins to rise high
The snow starts to melt and say goodbye.

Lauren Titera & Jessie-May Edmonds (11)
Ducklington CE Primary School

WEATHER

The cloud fell lower and lower
Over the climbing city,
The wind started to scream,
The hail grinned as it punched
Humans in the face,
The fog laughed as it stopped
People going out,
The rain jumped as it slapped the cars,
The arms of the sun cleared it all up.

Craig Tredwell (11)
Ducklington CE Primary School

TORNADO

The tornado comes from nowhere
Dancing round and round pulling off roofs
Like a baby with a doll's house
It whistles everywhere it goes
Snatching bricks and cars
Less mercy than a soldier with a gun
Shouts then disappears into the deep fog.

Sam Hatton (11)
Ducklington CE Primary School

TREASURE

Shining silver
Glimmering gold
Sparkly silk
Brown chest
Golden sand
Dazzling diamonds
Gleaming rubies
Precious plates
(Gold and silver.)

Harry Barlow (8)
Ewelme CE Primary School

JORDAN'S PET

Jordan had a pet snake
All the time he went to the lake
So Jordan took him to the vet
The vet said, 'This is one slithery pet!'

When the snake was on the table
The vet came in, he gave the snake a label
'Open wide,' said the vet
'You slithery, slippery pet.'

Jordan Goldspink (8)
Ewelme CE Primary School

JAMES' PET

James had a pet ant
But he was always in trouble
He couldn't drink blackcurrant
Because he popped every bubble

James took his ant
For a run
But the poor ant
Didn't have fun

James put his ant in the shed
But he blushed and went very red

So James took his ant
To the school
But everyone said, 'What a fool'

So James took his ant
To the cinema
But the ant ran to the bar

So James gave his ant a sweet
But his ant nearly lost his feet

So James, at last
Took his pet, very fast
To the vet.

Elspeth Walker (7)
Ewelme CE Primary School

ASHLEY'S PET

Ashley, a teenager, had a pet frog
But everywhere she took him
They got lost in the fog

One day she took him to the park
To have some fun
Then he got a disease
From a dirty, green bun

Ashley was worried
So she took him to the vet
As they went through the door
They got very wet

Whilst the vet was testing
Ashley hung her clothes to dry
But the vet was very clumsy
And poked the frog in the eye

Ashley put her clothes back on
And rushed her frog away
When she finally got home
It was nearly the next day

She took him to the pond
To try to make him ribbit
And when she came back
To her surprise, he actually did it!

She took him to the council
To see if he had lied
Then she went to get a drink
But when she came back
The poor frog had died.

Kia Little (8)
Ewelme CE Primary School

TREASURE

Shimmering sun
Shining sea
Singing seagulls
Palm trees

Sandy shores
Rusty chest
Silver, gold
Silken vest

Diamonds, coins
Rubies red
Cups, plates
Torn ted

Jewels, beads
Coins round
Picture frame
Golden crown

Beautiful crystals
Necklaces, pearls
Paper pens
Golden curls

Trophies, medals
Beads, aquamarine
Copper and bronze
Toy submarine

Great treasure
Swishing sea
Chocolate, sweets
For me!

Gemma Bolton (9)
Ewelme CE Primary School

CHEETAHS

Cheetahs,
Running swiftly,
Making dust fly behind,
Making its fur blow in the wind,
Cheetahs

Cheetahs,
Gigantic cats,
Pouncing on its prey,
Camouflaging itself in the grass,
Cheetahs

Cheetahs,
Eating red meat,
Just waiting to jump out,
Running at sixty miles an hour,
Cheetahs.

Elliott Sean Hughes (9)
Ewelme CE Primary School

FARMS

In the country
Smell of hay
In the yards, machines
Weighing scales for pigs
Around the yards are fields
Hay in barns
Keep it from the rain
Animals in fields
Trailers on tractors
Dogs barking
People working.

Jonathan Lansley (9)
Ewelme CE Primary School

SKY KENNING

White clouds,
Up high,
To reach,
Must fly.

Birds there,
All day,
Birds there,
To play.

So big,
Bright-blue,
So free,
Fly through.

Up there,
Plane goes,
So bright,
Never snows.

Jordan Watts (10)
Ewelme CE Primary School

TREASURES

T opaz
R uby
E merald
A mber
S apphire
U nder the sea
R ose quartz
E verything
S ilver.

Faron Watts (9)
Ewelme CE Primary School

BIMBO'S PET LIZARD

Bimbo was a funny clown
He bought a pet lizard
Bimbo called him Spotty Brown
He blew away in a blizzard

What the lizard didn't know
Was Bimbo was a wizard
The clown didn't tell anyone
And he magically made the lizard
Appear from the blizzard
The people outside shouted, 'Well done!'

'I am hungry,' said the lizard
So he had some mice
On the news it said
There would be no more blizzards
Bimbo just sat and played a game with a dice.

Laura Griffin (8)
Ewelme CE Primary School

JOHN'S PET

There lived a man called John
He had a pet lion
And he was upset
So they took him to the vet

He ate up the vet
What a funny pet!
Then through a snowy blizzard
Came a wicked wizard

The wizard said, 'Abra-a-doo
I sent the lion to the zoo!'
He met some lions in a huddle
But all they wanted was to cuddle.

Hayley Jameson (7)
Ewelme CE Primary School

WILLIAM'S PET

William's got a whale for a pet
She couldn't swim
She didn't like getting wet
So he took her to the vet

The vet said, 'Does she have her fish?'
'Yes, on her shiny dish.'
The vet went to a tank
The vet fell in and sank!

The vet touched something that dashed
He pulled out a fish that made a big splash
The whale ate the fish and William spent a lot of cash
The vet tipped something over that made a big crash

The vet gave him a pool
William took it home and they bathed in the cool
William went inside and brought out a stool
The whale thought he was a fool

William took her to the pier
They went on a boat and the whale could steer!
William went to the bar and he drank too much beer
When they got off the boat, they saw some deer.

Elizabeth Spence (7)
Ewelme CE Primary School

TREASURE

Shiny, sparkly
Rusty, dusty
As it could be
Old, creaky
Golden box
The rusty hinges
Wonderful, beautiful
Golden treasure
Green, red
Purple, blue
Brown, gold
Every colour that you can think of
Wonderful treasure
Beautiful treasure
Golden treasure
I love treasure.

Charlotte Moore (11)
Ewelme CE Primary School

CROCODILE

Thorny back,
River king,
River hunter,
Sudden beast,
Floating log,
Silent monster,
Snappy jaws,
Ancient animal,
Freshwater animal,
An amphibian.

Rose Parker (9)
Ewelme CE Primary School

MY TEDDY

Warm eyes
Soft paws
Lovely smile
What more?

Colourful coat
White frost
Short ears
Never lost

Soft toy
Long nose
Always together
Everyone knows

White fur
Squeeze tight
Loveable look
Night-night!

Bella Maine (8)
Ewelme CE Primary School

GOLD

Bright coins
Shiny metal
Hidden treasure
Bury the box
Deep underground
Putting the sand back
Filling in the hole.

Jack Eccles (9)
Ewelme CE Primary School

CITY CAT

Crawling sneakily
Cunningly clever
Dirty breath
Pouncing and prowling
Eating mice
Irritating a snail
Dodging cars
Hearing tyres screech
Jumping over fences
Searching for meat
Hissing loudly
Scaring off its prey
Eating out of dustbins
Climbing up trees
Jumping for birds
Catapulting down
Raerghhh!
Looking for danger
Bravely going on
Finding a warm place
Going to sleep.

Jessica Jewitt (11)
Ewelme CE Primary School

MY DOG

Smooth fur
As black as night
Always pleased to see you
Her long tail does not stop wagging
Molly
Getting
Ready for a walk
She is excited

Her long tail does not stop wagging
Molly
In the night
Her fur gleams
Shining in the moonlight
Her long tail does not stop wagging
Molly.

Olivia Stoddart (9)
Ewelme CE Primary School

BOATS

Breaking waves.
Gliding through.
Engines revving.
Water flying.
Exhausts smoking.
Propellers turning.
Distant rumble.
Diesel motors.
Never stopping.
Wind blowing.
Sails pushing.
People racing.
Ellen MacArthur.
World champion.
On Kingfisher.
Cruise liners.
Hovercrafts.
Long canoes.
Big barges.
On the sea.
On river.

David Granat (11)
Ewelme CE Primary School

BIRDS

Red kite
Swift mover
Mouse catcher
Its food

Male pheasant
Game bird
Shoot it
Hunt it

Crow, raven
Blackbird
Dark black
Horrible bird

All different
Some nice
Some horrible
All they want is food, food and food

In the winter
No food
Feed the birds all day long
I love my bird!

Trudy Jones (9)
Ewelme CE Primary School

CHEETAH

Spotted, fast
Leaper, sprinter
Jumper, hot
Furry, smooth
Quiet, patient
Silky, smooth

Big, scary
Sharp teeth
Spiky claws
Shining eyes
Sneaky mind
Raging, angry
Eats anything.

Fran Walker (8)
Ewelme CE Primary School

HIDDEN TREASURE

The brown, heavy treasure chest
Resting on the sand
The sparkly little jewels
Sitting on the chest
The breakable shining plates
Smacking on the wood
The glimmering light
Shining from the sun
The breakable rusty plates
Sitting in front of the blazing sun

The blazing sun
Shining on the chest
The small shiny diamonds
Sparkling in front of the chest
The pearls on the necklace
The small little coins
Scattered on the sand
The green big bottle
Stuck in the sand
The ripped old cloth
Jammed in the bottom of the chest.

Christopher Perkins (11)
Ewelme CE Primary School

GREETING CINQUAINS

Hello
Are you OK?
I am glad to see you
Come inside for something to drink
Bonjour!

Greetings
From me to you
I hope you will like it
Come inside for a while, sit down
Hola

Farewell
Do you have to?
I would like you to stay
I wish you didn't have to go
Away

Farewell
You're departing
Goodbye, you're leaving me
I have to say farewell, goodbye
Adieu.

Connie Jacobs (9)
Ewelme CE Primary School

TREASURE KENNING

Glistening key
Rusty lock
Shining gold
Beautiful doll
Glittering jewels
Magnificent silver

Royal crowns
Rubies red
Sapphires blue
Jewellery boxes
Made from
Diamonds galore.

Lucinda Kenrick (8)
Ewelme CE Primary School

RAINDROPS

Dripping from the gutters,
Shining in the bright sun,
Here comes the rainbow,
Now the rain's work is done.

Beaming in the sunshine,
Smiling at the rainbow,
Gleaming in the downpour,
The sun is being slow.

It's coming out again,
To see everyone,
Making everyone hope,
That here comes the sun.

But clinging to the pipes,
The raindrops shimmer bright,
Making people smile,
At least for a while,
Before rain comes again.

Chloe Maine (9)
Ewelme CE Primary School

STAG BEETLE

Sharp pincers,
Rough edge.
Scuttly feet,
In grass.
Beady eyes,
Shining bright.
Smooth shell,
Feeling great.
Small antennae,
Twitching fast.
Dark colour,
Like clouds.
Crushing prey,
Like teeth.
Hiding well,
In cracks.
With other
Fellow insects.
Fighting strong,
One lost,
Upside down.
Big wings,
Open up.
Fluttering away,
Like butterflies,
In the
Gusting wind.

Daniel Clements (11)
Ewelme CE Primary School

TREASURE

In the
Deep sand
By the
Seashore
Who knows
Where it
Is hidden?

Glistening gold
Shining silver
In an
Old chest
Worn out
Fragile sides
I open
It up . . .

On an
Old map
I see
The position
Of the
Old chest
In it
Is a
Silken dress
Satin shoes
And lots
Of jewels.

Jessica Griffin (8)
Ewelme CE Primary School

SUN

Shimmering light,
As magical as gold,
Ablaze in the bright sky,
A gleam of beauty,
Brightness in the air,
An amazing sight,
A wonderful feature,
A treasure up high
An attraction to the world,
A hot star,
A yellowy light,
A yellowy daylight,
As the day fades,
It disappears,
Until tomorrow.

Rosie Duffield (9)
Ewelme CE Primary School

RAINBOW CINQUAINS

Red, green
And indigo
Bright, beautiful colours
When it rains and the sun is bright
Look up

Colours
And all strange kinds
Bright sky, amazing high
It shimmers as the sun goes by
Precious.

Hannah Fitzgerald (9)
Ewelme CE Primary School

My Favourite Teddy

Really soft
Especially cute
Brownie fur
Tattered suit

Sits there
All day
Nobody else
To play

Stands there
Looks sad
I'm home
He's glad.

Jessica Veitch (10)
Ewelme CE Primary School

The Owl And The Tiger

The owl and the tiger went to sea
On an old plank of wood
The tiger ran around a lot
While the owl ate all he could
The owl looked up to the rain above
And sang to a rock guitar
Oh growling tiger how fierce you are
Oh look how fierce you are
They sailed away for half a day
Until they saw some land
There were palm trees and sunbathers
With lots and lots of sand.

Charlie Walker (10)
Ewelme CE Primary School

MY PUPPY

Rubies red
Sapphires blue
Inside the box
I found you

You're sweet and fluffy
Now I've got you
Sometimes annoying
Still, I love you

Cuddly, soft
Coat so pale
Sad-looking eyes
Wagging tail

When I am sad
You make me feel happy
A brown patch on your eye
You look so dappy

For a lopsided look
And a snow-white body
You look so cute
Against everybody

Sometimes get rough
So not as sweet
You like to get tough
So not as loving

You're pretty and soft
You smell like green grass
The one problem is
You won't let dogs pass

However much asked, I will not lend
Because you are my very best friend.

Ellie Clements (9)
Ewelme CE Primary School

TOM'S PET

Tom had a pet
Its name was Met
He had a sore limb
But it killed him

It was a fish
But after he made it into a dish
Soon he went to the pet shop
And he bought a pet named Hop

It was a moth
But it drank broth
And it was his pet
He called him Met

He took it for a run
But the moth did not have fun
He went to the vet
'Come in, Tom,' said the vet.

Rhys Thomas (7)
Ewelme CE Primary School

DANIEL'S PET

One day Daniel got a pet
He caught it in a net
Once he took it to the park
But when he got back, it was very dark

So Daniel took it to a sanctuary
But when he woke up
He found it was imaginary
Then he took it on an aeroplane
But he found it was not tame!

Daniel's pet was very naughty
And pecked at a bit of lemon curd
Daniel's pet is a *bird!*

Jack Ventress (8)
Ewelme CE Primary School

TREASURE

Shining brightly like the sun
Diamonds sharp as a thorn
Silver glinting like the moon's reflection
Sapphires as blue as the sea
Rubies as red as blood
Pearls as white as clouds
Silk as smooth as a snake
Gold plates just like a lion's mane
Jewels as beautiful as a fully grown rose
Cloth as soft as a bear's fur.

Alex Butler (11)
Ewelme CE Primary School

TREASURE

Deep, deep
Down in the sand,
Sparkling silver and
Glittering gold, will it be found?
Treasure.

Treasure,
Glittering so,
It is in the desert,
Did you know it is there? Of course
It's there.

See it,
Glistening so,
Can you see the locked chest?
Rubies red, so shiny and bright,
Glowing.

Elspeth Wilson (8)
Ewelme CE Primary School

DIAMONDS

Expensive jewels
Rarely found
Very valuable
Golden, silver
Sharp and see-through
Precious gem
Bright and strong
Small and shining
James Bond.

Kit Walker (8)
Ewelme CE Primary School

WATER

The glint of diamonds sprinkled across
on subtly faded beds of gravel
rushing to the mill that's proudly been
standing through the centuries

The calming background of chaotic water
a gorgeous patchwork duvet sky
the long river meandering, wandering
like a hungry, poor, lost cat

The wind skimming the river's surface
like an overflowing tap
the willow trees resting against
a lovely, wintry, breezy air.

Lizzy Ewers (10)
Hanney CE Primary School

THE COUNTRYSIDE

The shimmering river is bedded with gravel,
the glittering, shining surface of gold.
A parade of dazzling diamonds dancing.

Prints of willows in the glowing sky,
rough green bark on the tree stumps.
The trees staring over the wind-whipped
surface of the river.

A nervous cat wandering around,
swirling, twisting, chasing its tail.
Following the tranquil river
as it weaves through the fields.

Grace Culley (10)
Hanney CE Primary School

STREAM DANCER

Parading down the dancers come
Swirling, twirling to and fro
A mischievous wind shimmers the surface
Beneath a translucent cloud-patched sky
It races the smooth river on.
Silhouettes of elderly willows
Meet the silky bright sky
And all the while glinting and shining
The dancers are waltzing on
Prowling and slinking the swift slender froth
Woven in patterns of ages,
Are quickly passing a cold winter wasteland
Plagued by the season of frost
And then . . . down to the sea . . . down . . . down
Down where it's destined to go
Down to the sea . . . down . . . down
Down where the rivers are lost . . .

Isobel Gahan (10)
Hanney CE Primary School

STRANGE AND WEIRD

One oblong, orange oil painting oddly,
Two tiny tins toppling tiredly,
Three twitching trucks tottering traditionally,
Four fuzzy felines fouling frequently,
Five frisky foals fidgeting foolishly,
Six sad sardines shaking severely,
Seven safe snakes saluting sadly,
Eight excellent escalators estimating evenly,
Nine nasty newts navigating nervously,
Ten tense toilet rolls telling tearfully.

Robyn Dark (10)
Hanney CE Primary School

RIVER

The twinkling flow of tranquil silence
Surrounded by swamp-green willows
Water clear like glinting glass
Speeding, darting, curling past
Whirling current, bubbling brook
Hikers stop to take a look.

Andrew Hughes (10)
Hanney CE Primary School

THE RIVER

Sunlight dances
On the gleaming water
With dashing fish swimming around
Raindrops fall and makes ripples on the water
Current blowing leaves to the shore
And the tranquil silence of willows swaying.

Jack Tokelove (9)
Hanney CE Primary School

CALMNESS

Calm, shady sky patched, undisturbed peacefulness
'Little whirlpool twist around and bubble slowly up'
Calm water flows tranquilly round
Welcome brightness peeping through trees
Melancholy echoing wind whistles past.

Emma Rebeckah Richens (10)
Hanney CE Primary School

RIVER POEM

Smooth sheets of smoky glass
Sliding on the river bed
Sweeping the air like shiny gold
A shadow or lava grinding down stones
Glistening sparks floating in the air
Like pure diamonds reflecting.

Brett Sawyer (10)
Hanney CE Primary School

THUNDER AND LIGHTNING

Rain taps on the window
Then a big flash, then a noise
People in their beds
Dogs are barking at the noise
Then the storm is all over.

Lisa Little (9)
Hanney CE Primary School

MY HAMSTER

He runs really fast
He spins round in his wheel
Gets dizzy quite fast
My hamster lives in a cage
In my bedroom, on my shelf.

Becky Aram (9)
Hanney CE Primary School

The End Of Winter

The end of winter
Sunny days
A dazzling reflection of the sun
The water spitting froth and spray
Clear water like bottle glass
With lots of people striding past
With a wind-woven surface
Like a transparent blanket
Raging through the rocks and woods
Into the murky, salty sea
Blue sky appearing
The winter mess is clearing
All the children come out to play
Because the winter is disappearing
The water gleams in the sun
Like diamonds imbedded in the gravel
Then all the people start to travel.

Edward Haynes (9)
Hanney CE Primary School

Outdoors

Dazzling sun sparkles on shadowed water
Glistening and glowing
Reflections of the bare trees in the water
Shimmering and shining

The sky patched with dusty clouds
Breezy and chilly
River rippling and twisting in the breeze
Draughty but sunny

Elegant countryside, peaceful and calm
Bright but windy
There's a mill tall, strong, with red bricks
Big and old.

Imogen Stringfellow (9)
Hanney CE Primary School

THE RIVER

A frothy, frosty, foaming bath
Like shadowed dancers on a gravely bed
Kicking up an icy spray
At a dark dancing disco
The wolf wind is music
Twisting, turning cheerfully
With a patchwork sky above them
The gentle flow of the calm water
Squirrels climb the bare trees
Getting sleepy
Turning into still glass
Sinking,
Sinking,
Gone
Forever.

Sarah Cornish (9)
Hanney CE Primary School

THE RIVER

The sun came shining over hills
Light beams of rays on water
Fish battling current furiously pike
Eating prey then suddenly silence.

Christopher Sellwood (11)
Hanney CE Primary School

RIVER

The twinkling flow of tranquil silence
Surrounded by green swooped willows
Clear water like glinting glass
Speeding, darting, curling past
Whirling current, bubbling brook
Hikers stop to take a look
The magnificent, brilliant, big, blue sky
Watching birds as they fly by.

Lawrence Stringfellow (11)
Hanney CE Primary School

WINTER

Murky, shifting, rippling,
Stream shining like a light beam.
Dazzling birds tweeting,
Peacefully a cat comes
And licks his lips tastefully.

Adrian Pepler (9)
Hanney CE Primary School

TIDAL WAVE

Tidal wave coming
Rolling forward to swamp town
People run in terror
The wave comes thundering down
The end of another town.

Joe Griffiths (10)
Hanney CE Primary School

RIVERS

The chilly breeze rushing through the air
The glistening sun rushing through the air with care
The dazzling river shining from the sun
The sea rushing down the brook
The curling river rushing with care.

David Eltham (10)
Hanney CE Primary School

CAMPFIRE

The fire is a terrifying human,
Toes and fingers,
Dancing about in the moonlight,
Bones crackle under his hair,
Toenails spit,
The glowing brain disintegrates,
The blood cools to a powdery mass.

Robin Styles (10)
John Hampden Primary School

THE BONFIRE

The burning fire is an angry person,
Reaching up to the sky with his slick, pointy fingers.
The sparkly hair falls to the ground lighting up the grass.
The hair like clouds, floats to the sky.
The bed of wood beneath his feet shrivelling and burning up.
Its glowing body, dancing around and around.

Jonathan McIver (11)
John Hampden Primary School

BONFIRE

Small whilst silently singing
Before the audience of flames
His legs crossed
A layer of ash strewn upon them

The glowing glare lighting up his face
Body straight with dignity
He sings a hushed melody
Whilst eyes dying
Dying into the ash
Of his blanket

Eventually the eyes close
The humming edges away
Waiting to come again.

Emily Moore (10)
John Hampden Primary School

BONFIRE

A bonfire is a raging person in prison.
Fingers trying to grab me
And put me under a spell.
Arms scattering,
To find more food.
Wood is its possession that keeps it alive,
But when the sun comes up,
It walks into a dark room
And never returns.

Louise Gibbons (10)
John Hampden Primary School

FIRE BEAST

The fire is a beast,
It creeps along the floor like a snake in the jungle,
It speaks like a toucan with his crackling sound,
Against everything it will win the battle of weapons.

Its fiery fingers climbing up the night sky,
Eyes watching, watching as they spring up into the air,
Glaze of light shining as the moon rises.

He is a new life, born to be free,
No one can stop him,
No one can betray him,
Apart from his kind.

His final hour is here,
He is resting, he is wounded,
He says these words before he flees
'I am the fire, I'm going back
But for the day, we will attack!'

Hannah Beaugeard (10)
John Hampden Primary School

HAIKUS

Cascading down rocks
Jumping up the sandy banks
Shining in the sun

Rushing down, in, out
Swirling all around the rocks
Lapping up the banks.

Maisie Faulkner (10)
John Hampden Primary School

The Escape

Faster than lightning,
No stuttering, stumbling,
Away, away I flee,
Before they catch me.

Escaped! I'm free!
Speeding down towards the sea,
Cascading down the mountain steep,
Plunging in the river deep.

Quickly winding through the rushes,
Whispering sounds and piercing hushes,
Round, down, in, out,
Curling all about.

I am there, my destiny,
To the freedom called the sea,
Catch me they will never,
For I go on forever.

Laura Dixon (10), Christopher Anderson,
Mitchell Meredith & Maisie (11)
John Hampden Primary School

The Volcano

As they walk to reach their destination
They hear a giant *bang*
As thunder claps and the sun fades
They keep on walking; they rest as it gets warmer
They look up and see red-hot liquid running down
As they stand it gets closer, until they give out a
Very high-pitched *scream!*
They never reach their destination.

Ina Coyle (11)
John Hampden Primary School

The Escape

Faster, faster
No stuttering, stumbling
Away, away I flee
Before they can catch me

Escaped! I'm free!
Into the open, towards the Atlantic sea
My heart pounding like a drum
Looking over my shoulder
As I run, run, run

I'm free, I'm free, no one has caught me
Sailing towards the deep blue sea.

Toby Maddox, Billy Wagerfield (10),
Kirsty Clarke & Justyn Reed (11)
John Hampden Primary School

The Bonfire

Fire is an angry person,
Waiting to escape,
Flames are his fingers,
Which dance like the wind,
Smoke are its arms which
Sway across the sky.
Wood under his feet are
The bed on which he lays,
Sparks simmer as they light the ground.
He comes to his end
And all that are left are his
Arms waving goodbye.

Stephen Price (10)
John Hampden Primary School

BONFIRE

It is a cold night but
I am warm,
Fingers moving about,
My hair is changing,
Red, orange, yellow.
Breath is ascending,
Bright eyes glancing,
Legs burning,
Breathing heavily,
Fingers up dancing.

I'm starting to die,
Silently I burn down, down.
Water is being pounded on me,
I descend,
I am cold.

Adam Clark (11)
John Hampden Primary School

A BONFIRE

A bonfire's ginger fingers
Can jump out
At any time,
Eyes are glowing,
He's watching my every move,
To keep him going
Feed him big, brown chocolate bars,
He lights up too
And puffs smoke out at you.

Kirsty Smith (10)
John Hampden Primary School

THE BONFIRE

I lay asleep,
A pile of sticks and twigs and other bits,
A match is lit and thrown on me,
Waking me from my sleep,
I see my arms catching alight
And suddenly glowing bright,
I reach my crackling hands up high,
I nearly touch the sky.

The wind starts to whistle,
The flames all twizzle
Down into a tiny flicker,
Pile of ashes growing thicker.

Now I am asleep again,
I'll wake up in the morning,
Then I'll burn any I desire,
For nothing is hotter than fire!

Zoë Francis (11)
John Hampden Primary School

BONFIRE

I am touching the sky.
The flames are my fingers,
Smoke is my hair.
Ashes are my feet,
Glowing eyes towards the light;
Sparkling as ever,
Taken like a bonfire.

Nicole Blanco (10)
John Hampden Primary School

I Went To The Future

I went to the future,
There was chocolate grass.
No glass on the ground.
Bubblegum hedges,
That blow automatic bubbles.
Balloons that lift you off the ground.
Caramel clothes, you can eat them at the cinema.
Vegetables that taste like Galaxies.

Living paper and houses.
Aliens come to Earth,
We become slaves on a world that has
Never been named or seen.
Ghosts come out of
Sewerage pipes.
The Earth explodes.

Lisa Thomas (8)
John Hampden Primary School

The Grass!

The grass is like waves,
clashing into the shore.
It slithers along like a snake,
crawling along the sand.
The grass grows long,
so long, like hair.
Then you go and have it cut,
by sharp blades.

Lucy Hearn (11)
John Hampden Primary School

THE BLUE GALLOPERS

The soft blue gallopers
With their silky, fine manes
Slowly approaching the shore
Jumping up and down

When they approach the shore
They wash out all the golden sand
Charging backwards to the sea
They hit the bottom and rise again

The wet washed-up beach
Waiting for the blue gallopers
To come charging back to shore
While the sun hides away

Now the sun is going down
The blue gallopers have to be calm
They softly stop their charging around
Ready not to make a sound.

Abi Mansfield (9)
John Hampden Primary School

BONFIRE

The tall bonfire
Dancing around
Temperature rising
Flames like arms
Splashing heat, moving faster
Reaching the gloomy skies
Ashes like cut hair
Scattered across the ground.

Daniel Hamp (11)
John Hampden Primary School

The Sun

The sun sneaks
Singing with puffed cheeks
Sun rips tops off
In delight
Sun relaxes, sunbathes
On the smiley beach
Sun makes shadows
On the droopy mountains.

Robert Rees (8)
John Hampden Primary School

A Journey Into Space

The walk of life
Was taken into our hands
To see a place of fantasy
Where no one has ever journeyed to before
A land of secrets, silence and adventure
The count was over in ten seconds
And we were in space.

Thomas Merriman (11)
John Hampden Primary School

Hot And Cold

Hot and humid
Frosty and freezing
That's the weather

Boiling and baking
Snowy and shivery
That's the weather

It's getting hot
It's getting cold
That's the weather
Always changing.

Rebecca Hickling (10)
John Hampden Primary School

AT THE DRAGON INFANT SCHOOL

Dragon infants
Hang their coats on dragon pegs
And sit on a dragon mat
In the corner
To have their dragon names called out.
The dragon teacher says,
'Now then little dragons,
Today we'll have a story about children!'

The little dragons chuckle,
Because they don't
Believe in children.
Sometimes they dress up
In the dragon playhouse
And have little dragon squabbles,
Which the dragon teacher has to sort out.
They learn
Lots of dragon games
And sing dragon songs
And if they tumble over
In the dragon playground,
They cry dragon tears,
Till Mum comes
To take them home.

Nick Palfrey (10)
John Hampden Primary School

THE BONFIRE

A bonfire is a lonely human;
Long and thin,
Creeps around every night,
His wide long fingers,
Glowing eyes in the mist beyond the moon,
His clashing teeth glow in the dark,
The clouds roar,
The giant moans the strangest tones,
His legs slip away from each other,
His arms pound at one another,
He is sinking down,
All that is left of him are burnt sticks.

Anna Howarth (10)
John Hampden Primary School

BONFIRE

The bonfire is a dancer,
Dancing in the wind.
Ashes are his eyes,
Logs are his feet.
Whirling, twirling in the wind,
The fire shakes his hands,
Jumping, prancing
And soaring up high.

The fire dies down,
He begins to bow,
The performance comes to a finish.

Wilber Sears (11)
John Hampden Primary School

THE RUSH HOUR

The plane is landing . . . it's landed,
Rush to get on,
There's too many people there,
Children get squashed,
The plane leaves.

The sea's clashing against the weather-worn rocks,
It sounds as though it's a mix of sounds of the sea,
Suddenly there's a glint on the horizon, getting nearer,
A clash of blue and green
And towering over us as if we were ants,
Above the huge image of a yeti,
Everything goes blue, black, green.

Dominic Stanway-Williams (10)
John Hampden Primary School

MY CAT

Black and white, clever and strong,
In his James Bond-like suit.
His weapon, his versatile claws,
His enemy the mice.
Stalking in the dark,
Hiding in the trees.
Trying not to be seen.
In the day he is practically harmless,
But at night he's a killing machine.
So people don't know who he is,
He has a code name - Double O Cat!

Ben Lindsay (11)
John Hampden Primary School

My Poem On Rivers

Rivers, rivers, how should I describe them?
Rivers, rivers, I could use personification
And create two river men.

As they wake up early in the morning,
They hold tight for a rippling ride,
Down the winding waterfall,
As if a crooked stair
And down again, still soaring,
The cliff made into an exciting slide,
That makes these men splash up high into the air.

The afternoon has now come,
The water has slowed down some,
These massive puddles just floating past,
Sailing like a ship but without sail or mast
And now the sun sets over them,
These tired-looking river men.

Swifter still into the night,
Stars above them shining bright,
Almost home, the place to rest,
That place that they know the best,
Out through the opened mouth,
They won't drift either north nor south,
They are back to the beginning of the cycle, sea!

Vicky Plater (10)
John Hampden Primary School

Snow

Snow frosts icy winter,
it slices red autumn.

Snow freezes cool spring,
it covers over hot summer.

Snow drifts down a mountain,
it settles cold and stiff.

Snow gives its last sigh and dies,
for the fight is over, summer won.

Helena Byrne-Stevens (9)
John Hampden Primary School

GUINEA PIGS' BATH

Guinea pigs itching, scratch, scratch, scratch
Time for a bath, splash, splash, splash
Wriggling, squeaky, not much fun!
Glad when it's over, get the job done!

Eardrops, mite spray, out with the brush
Eyes wide, nose twitching, ears upright
Really not happy, watch out they might bite
Give them a huge big fuss

Bubbles bubbling everywhere
Give them a wash, if you dare!
Nearly done, a good job too
Water on the floor, bubbles in your hair

Whip the towel out
They might get a chill
Rub, rub, rub, till they are dry
Their wet, shiny hair in the sunlight

Back in the cage, lots of extra hay
Have a special treat, yes you may
Clean, fresh, fluffy, happy and carefree
I love you, you love me!

Amanda Rawlings (10)
John Hampden Primary School

THE MAGIC MAN

The magic man has magic clothes, he plays a tune on his magic flute
From his tiny pocket flies out a cat
Then from his black hat pops out a rat

Then with his magic guitar he makes himself a star
Then he puts a person in a box
And says, 'You will become a fox!'

His big hands make tiny little cards flitter around
Then magic coins trickle down to the ground
Now that's a magic man!

George White (9)
John Hampden Primary School

TREASURE HUNT

Come to Treasure Island
And we'll find some lovely gold

We'll build a big sandcastle
And we'll dig for chests of gold

I am sure we'll find some jewels
Diamonds, rubies and pearls

I've got my secret treasure map
So let's get digging girls.

Laura Elliott (8)
John Hampden Primary School

THE BONFIRE

The bonfire is like a gentle person,
He waved through the midnight sky,
Lighting all around him.
On the ground his coaly feet,
The cranky, burning, wooden legs,
High and forlorn,
Flames were flailing,
Arms in the breeze.
Tiny, white tips for fingers,
Smoke rising, shaped a handsome face,
Rain fell and slowly the fire fell too.

Luke Ounsworth (10)
John Hampden Primary School

THE SNOW

now crunches
On wriggling dustbins.
Snow freezes
Icy breaths.
Snow breathes
Down shivering fires.
Snow covers
Creeping houses.
Snow floats down,
It will be back again.

Ben Carrington (9)
John Hampden Primary School

STORM

The storm goes clutter
And the birds won't flutter
Boom, boom, boom
And a bang
The storm goes crash
And it makes a flash
Boom, boom, boom
And a bang.

Elena Rees (10)
John Hampden Primary School

SEPTEMBER 11TH

The world went silent as the true disaster struck,
I thought it was a film, but it dawned on me
That is was real.

All those innocent people dying,
Fighting for their lives,
This life-taking war cannot go on.

Emily Braund (11)
John Hampden Primary School

WAR

War is not fair
People crying in despair

War is a battle you have to face
Aeroplanes and boats in a chase

War is extremely bad
Families broken and sad

Many countries die and fail
I wish war was a fairytale.

Annabel Grace (9)
John Hampden Primary School

FIRE

The fire is me,
Orange and red,
Blazing in the sky,
Burn . . . burn . . . burn!

Fed by my parents
To survive,
I lay
As my spirits go,
Ashes . . . ashes . . . ashes!

Ross McGoun (11)
John Hampden Primary School

TESSA

My puppy's all skinny and fluffy,
She's black and her tail's all tufty,
She's got long collie hair
And she bites like a bear,
She sits in the kitchen
And nibbles the chairs,
She's got teeth like needles
And is as naughty as a weasel!

Jessica Evans (10)
John Hampden Primary School

BONFIRE

Bonfire, bonfire;
Arise,
Awaken,
Climb up, up, up,
The dead sacrificed branches
With your flickering, flamed arms,
Hands burning in fiery fingers
Which devour, devour, devour.

Crackling,
Popping,
Your sound, your sound,
Your sound is one of a firework
Crackling in the distance.

Your ash,
Your ash follows down your fingers,
Dancing around,
Scars of the past.

A distinctive smell,
Unique as a fingerprint
Of a human.

Your flame will die,
Die down,
Do not be filled with woe,
Further your flame will go,
Further your flame will last
Not as vicious as in the past,
Burn, deep down in your heart,
A memorial flame,
In an era will grow again.

Sofie Jones (11)
John Hampden Primary School

INVISIBLE FRIEND

My four invisible friends are very special
You would probably think that's quite a lot
They stay with me all day

Sometimes they fly in the wind
And sometimes they annoy me!
Rachel (that's one of 'em) wants to be an actress
Once Lilly flew away and didn't come back
Until the next day!
But they're all my friends and that's what counts.

Isabella Whiteman (9)
John Hampden Primary School

TIGER

I'm a tiger trapped in metal
I used to pounce from here to there
I think nobody likes me
And nobody cares
I'm a tiger trapped in metal
And now I feel alone and sad
I try to remember
The good times I had
I'm a tiger trapped in metal
In the jungle I used to play
We did lots of things
In just one day
I'm a tiger trapped in metal
I'm dying, I'm dying
Please help me
Because I'm crying.

Daniel Ferguson (9)
Millbrook CP School

I Am A Monkey

I am a monkey,
Trapped in a cage,
I am homesick and bored,
In a boring old cage.

Cold and shiny
Are the bars of the cage,
Slippery and slidey
Are the bars of the cage.

I am a monkey,
Trapped in a cage,
I am homesick and bored,
In a boring old cage.

Swinging on a rope,
Instead of jungle trees,
Beady eyes are staring
At the other monkeys and me.

I am a monkey,
Trapped in a cage,
I want to be free,
From this boring old cage.

Thomas Smith (9)
Millbrook CP School

Up In The Attic, Down In The Cellar

Something's smelling in the dark, dusty chairs
An old rusty bike
Broken-down train set
An old shabby book
An old fishing kit

Rusty old tools
A mucky, dusty, broken high chair
Broken chairs
A moist J-cloth
A dark shadow
In the corner and something's breathing.

Declan Laycock (10)
Millbrook CP School

I AM A MONKEY

I am a monkey,
I live in a zoo,
I want to be free,
Just like you.

I miss all my family,
My sister and mother,
My granny and grandad,
My dad and my brother.

I am a monkey,
I live in a zoo,
I want to be free,
Just like you.

I don't like it here,
The fountains are oozing,
I don't eat at all,
I am just snoozing.

I am a monkey,
I have a great rage,
My life's been so boring,
Cos I'm in a *cage!*

Daniel Pope (9)
Millbrook CP School

I AM A MONKEY

I'm a monkey,
I live in a zoo,
I've got nothing to do,
All I see is people looking at me.

I'm a monkey,
I live in a cage,
What an outrage,
I hate this metal cage.

I'm a monkey,
I used to swing,
But now my ears ring,
At the noise in the zoo.

I'm a monkey,
All I've got is a hollow log,
I remember the misty fog
In the peaceful, pleasant forest.

I'm a helpless monkey,
I live in a zoo,
I have nothing to do,
What shall I do?

George Jackson (9)
Millbrook CP School

LOVE

Love is the colour of cherry blossom
It sounds like the beautiful songs of the birds of love
A group of humming birds singing their sweet songs
Love feels like a dream, like your heart is melting

Love smells like the blessed red roses
Love tastes like juicy red strawberries
Fresh from a bush in the summer sun
It lives in the lovely land of Eden.

Ashley Ward (10)
Millbrook CP School

I AM A BUTTERFLY

I am a butterfly
With my lovely wings
Patterned with spots
And other lovely things

I am a butterfly
High in the air
Flying so high
I don't really care!

I am a butterfly
Landing on the grass
Daisies and other flowers
I flutter off but not fast

I am a butterfly
Crashing into the rain
It's dropping on my wings
I can feel the pain

I am a butterfly
Hiding in the tree
All wet and dripping
And then I snuggle up
And go to sleep in a patch of leaves.

Hayley Chapman (9)
Millbrook CP School

DEATH

Death is night-black,
It smells like rotten fish,
Death tastes cruel and sour,
It sounds like nails on a misty blackboard,
It feels slimy and cold,
Death lives in the heart of a graveyard.

Liam Smith (10)
Millbrook CP School

PAIN

Pain is blood-red,
It smells like hot lava,
Pain tastes spicy and boils,
It sounds like the screeches of a blackboard,
It feels as sharp as knives,
Pain lives in caves of darkness.

Joe Braham (10)
Millbrook CP School

PAIN

Pain is dark red
It smells like fumes
Pain tastes as bitter as coldness
It sounds like piercing screams
Pain feels like a hot iron pressing on your skin
Pain lives in the heart of our souls.

Jamie Burton (10)
Millbrook CP School

ABSTRACT NOUNS POEM

Disease is dark green
It smells like damp compost
Disease tastes like sour lemon
It sounds like the wind moaning
It feels rough like pebbles
Disease lives in the deep ocean.

Jessica Peart (10)
Millbrook CP School

JOY

Joy is bright yellow,
It smells like a spring morning,
Joy tastes like chocolate ice cream,
It sounds like children shouting,
It feels warm and soft,
Joy lives in a theme park.

Jennifer Douch (9)
Millbrook CP School

JOY

Joy is sunny yellow
Joy smells like beautiful scented roses
Joy tastes like sweet, ripe fruit
Joy sounds like chirpy birds at sunrise
Joy feels like fluffy kittens
Joy lives in good news.

Emily Steven-Fountain (10)
Millbrook CP School

I Am A Dolphin

I'm a dolphin,
Stuck in a tangly net,
All I can do is squeak,
Whine and maybe even swear.

I am a dolphin stuck in a tangly net

I'm a dolphin,
Stuck in a tangly net,
I wish I was free to swim,
Jump and paddle about.

I am a dolphin stuck in a tangly net.

I'm a dolphin,
Stuck in a tangly net,
I wish,
I wish,
I wish,
I was *free!*

Katie Evans (9)
Millbrook CP School

Disappointment

Disappointment is the colour of a teardrop,
Disappointment smells like chips that have been burnt.
Disappointment tastes dry and dirty.
Disappointment sounds like a smouldering fire.
Disappointment feels hard and flattening.
Disappointment lives in the heart of you!

Katie-May Boulter (10)
Millbrook CP School

I Am A Shark

I am a shark,
Dying on the shore,
I don't have my family,
With me anymore.

I used to swim with
All my best friends,
But now I'm here,
My life's about to end.

I am a shark,
Dying on the shore,
I don't have my family,
With me anymore.

I used to glide,
Through reef and bays,
All my best friends,
Would want to play.

I am a shark,
Dying on the shore,
I don't have my family,
With me anymore.

I screech, I wail
And I swear like mad,
I said some things
I shouldn't had.

But I can't do
Anything more,
As I'm a shark,
Dying on the shore.

Georgina Naish (10)
Millbrook CP School

I Am A Pig

I am a pig
In a stinky place
I've always got mud
Smeared on my face

I used to have
A family
That was the time
I was free

I am a pig
In a stinky place
I've always got mud
Smeared on my face

I was playing
In the grass
When someone grabbed me
He was really fast

I am a pig
In a stinky place
I've always got mud
Smeared on my face

The mudbath here
Is not as good as at home
Wherever I am
Everywhere here is where I'm alone

I am a pig
In a stinky place
I've always got mud
Smeared on my face

What are these humans doing to me
I try very hard to flee, flee, flee.

Luke Dady (9)
Millbrook CP School

ANGER

A nger is Dad having a bad day at work
N ever, ever stops having lots of paperwork
G etting closer and closer
E levating up the elevator
R un! Dad's coming!

Lewis Goulding (10)
Millbrook CP School

JOY

The colour of joy makes a rainbow
It tastes like freshly-baked cakes
It feels like the hot sun shining on a yellow field of daffodils
It smells like a valley of truly smelling flowers
It sounds like birds singing on a fine summer's day
Joy lives in the heart of every living soul.

Samantha Boardman (9)
Millbrook CP School

DEATH

Death is scalding lava burning away at your body
It smells like dead bodies and rotten fish
Death tastes like maggots crawling down your throat
It sounds like mountains crushing in your ears
It feels like vampires sucking the blood out of your neck
Death lives in the deepest, darkest, creepiest part of a volcano.

Tom Bennett (10)
Millbrook CP School

DEATH

Death's colour is ash-black.
Death tastes like your own skin.
Death feels like nothing but your heart has past on.
Death smells like gravel in your body.
Death sounds like the scream of terror.
Death lives in your own soul.

James Lloyd (9)
Millbrook CP School

JOY

Joy is happiness through the air
Joy smells like sweet roses
It tastes like sour sweets
Joy is all the bright colours of the rainbow
It feels like bubbling liquid inside you
Joy lives in a bright poppy field.

Sheridan Hetherington (10)
Millbrook CP School

HAPPINESS

Happiness is the brightest of reds
It smells like freshly-fallen snow
Happiness tastes like a delicious home made mince pie
It sounds like children playing with their new toys
Happiness feels like a soft snowflake floating into your hands
It lives in the heart of everyone.

Adam Badger (9)
Millbrook CP School

DEATH

Death is deep red like the centre of the Earth,
It smells like boiling, bubbling lava,
It tastes like cold, salty liquid freezing over,
It sounds like a stream of blood trickling through your veins,
Death feels like a knife piercing through your heart,
Death lives at the bottom of a gravestone.

Hal Davison (9)
Millbrook CP School

HAPPINESS

Happiness is the colour of bright-red,
It smells like bursting strawberries,
Happiness tastes like a chocolately mini Vienetta,
It sounds like a beautiful magic harp,
Happiness feels like a smooth silk coat,
It lives in the soul of loving children.

Lewis King (10)
Millbrook CP School

JOY

Joy is the colour of the bright red-hot sun in the shining sky
Joy lives in the heart of an angel
Joy feels as soft as a fluffy feather
Joy sounds like the hatching of a baby chick
Joy tastes like a sweet and juicy orange
Joy smells like a piece of chocolate melting in a pan.

Christina Wilkinson (10)
Millbrook CP School

LOVE

Love is the colour of a pink bow tied round a present.
It sounds like a sweet hum of a humming bird.
It feels like the soft fur of a teddy bear.
It smells like gigantic muffins baking.
It tastes like gooey chocolates melting in your mouth.
It lives in the deep soul of someone's heart.

April Haynes (9)
Millbrook CP School

ANGER

Anger is the colour of hot, steaming crimson.
Anger sounds like a war has just begun.
Anger feels like you have cut yourself to see how much it bleeds.
Anger smells like a bad-tempered lion.
Anger tastes like gone off beer in a sewage can.
Anger lives in the soul of your heart.

Declan Dorsett (10)
Millbrook CP School

DEATH

Death tastes like blood being sucked up and spat out again.
Death smells like it's come from an angry person.
Death's colour is like red-hot burning lava.
Death sounds like coal falling through a hollow bone.
Death feels like your heart being pulled out of a socket.
Death lives in the heart of a hollow skull.

Sean Finegan (10)
Millbrook CP School

DEATH

Death is black as coal.
Death smells like sizzling, scorching blood.
Death sounds like the screaming of Ork.
Death tastes like lava slithering down your throat.
Death feels like blades slashing into your flesh.
Death lives in the Temple of Doom.

Barney Gill (9)
Millbrook CP School

HAPPINESS

Happiness is the colour of the bright sun.
Happiness is the smell of roses.
Happiness is the shape of a face smiling.
Happiness is the taste of Dairy Milk chocolate.
Happiness is made by children having fun.
Happiness lives in a bright garden full of roses.

Jodi Wallbridge-Marshall (9)
Millbrook CP School

JOY

Joy smells like candy
and looks like all the
colours of the rainbow.
It tastes like all the
nicest sweets possible.
It sounds like children playing.
It feels comfy and pleasurable.
Joy lives in the candy-full
Heart of a child.

Tommy Courtney (10)
Millbrook CP School

HAPPINESS

Happiness is bright-blue like a summer sky with cotton clouds.
Happiness is like fresh flowers.
Happiness tastes like ice cream with all the toppings.
Happiness sounds like children playing on a bouncy castle.
Happiness feels like playing with your friends.
Happiness lives in the middle of everyone.

Martyn Lucas (10)
Millbrook CP School

HAPPINESS

Happiness has all the colours of the rainbow.
Happiness smells like fresh wind blowing in the trees.
Happiness sounds like the tweeting of baby birds in the sun.
Happiness feels like a cat's fur that's just been groomed.
Happiness lives in a heart of a baby hamster.

Naomi Swinney (10)
Millbrook CP School

DOLPHIN

I am a dolphin trapped in a stingy net
I used to swim all night and all day
I used to sing beautiful songs
In the cool blue water I used to play

I am a dolphin trapped in a stingy net
I miss the succulent fish I used to graze
I miss the blissful friends
I miss the splattering waves

I am a dolphin not free anymore
I am stuck in a scanty pool
For plenty of people to adore.

Shelley Syme (9)
Millbrook CP School

THE BRAVE ALSATIAN

One dark, cold night an Alsatian broke loose,
While running round town in darkness
He heard a faint cry,
He leapt around the corner spying a burglar in the distance,
Holding a gun up high, a bag of money in the other hand,
He sensed, as a dog of brown and cream would,
Something was wrong, so he went to set it right,
He chased the criminal round town until one fatal leap,
The burglar fell to the ground in pain,
Once the criminal was in prison
And a prisoner for the rest of his life,
All the money back in the bank,
The Alsatian is the hero of that day.

Lewis Butler (9)
Millbrook CP School

UNHAPPY MONKEY

I am an unhappy monkey,
I live in a great big zoo,
Trying to remember
All the things I used to do.
When it starts to rain,
I get this funny pain,
That's when I get sad,
I begin to get quite mad.
I am an unhappy monkey,
I live in a great big zoo,
Trying to remember
All the things I used to do.
I used to swing quite freely,
Amongst the summer trees,
My mummy used to help scratch
All them bad, bad fleas.
Now I have to peel bananas by myself,
When the zoo manager, that small little elf
Just chucks them over the gate.
I am an unhappy monkey,
I live in a great big zoo,
Trying to remember
All the things I used to do.

Jamie Hickman (9)
Millbrook CP School

BEAUTIFUL FISH

How the fish reflect the sunlight on their beautiful scales
Lying motionless as a whale or a shark swims by
Darting through the lovely light-blue water
With their tails trailing behind like a beautiful long kite
How the dolphins emit songs which make you stop what you are doing

As it washes out the bad things and puts you down to sleep
I wonder? I wonder how big fish grow?
How small fish glimmer?
And yes, they are so pretty
I'd love to be a fish.

Henry Anderson Elliott (8)
New College School

OLD AGE

Oh I wish I wasn't old
You are scared, in pain and wobbly
You're bent, twisted and clumsy
You're trapped inside your ancient body
Oh I wish I wasn't old

You're embarrassed sometimes
And you're fumbly and forgetful
You can't run or play outside
Oh I wish I wasn't old

Oh you're hunched and frail
You are near to dying
You need someone to help you go in and out the bath
But you can listen to your grandson or your grandaughter
And give advice to them
But I still wish I wasn't old

You can't go up and down the stairs
Or play tag or football
If you drop things you can't pick them up again
You're confused and wrinkled
Oh I wish I wasn't old.

James Millard (9)
New College School

UNDER THE WATER AND ON THE BEACH

Dive under the water deep, deep down
See how peaceful it all is
Be cautious of the dangerous fish
You never know what there might be
There might even be octopuses trailing
Lots and lots of lovely glittery legs
Hiding stingrays camouflaged against the grey rocks
And lovely starfish which are glittery
Go to the shipwrecks which have sunk down
See how the coral is all around you
And the bright colours, orange, green and blue
Look at the birds swim for fishes
When the birds go deep, deep down
The birds get killed by sea snakes hiding in the coral
Then washes the rubbish, pollution like bags
They can't live with it and then the lovely, lovely
Birds fly and fly into the bags and peck and swallow them!
And then they die
Poor, poor animals which live in the sea
And poor birds suffocating.

Clym Buxton (8)
New College School

OH HOW I WISH

I wish I could run and jump and play,
I wish I could just run away
From this ancient body.
Oh how I wish.
I wish I could hear and see,
I wish I could play in the sea,
Away from this old age.
Oh how I wish.

I used to have lots of friends,
Now I am lonely,
I wish I had someone to talk to.
Oh how I wish.
I used to be handsome,
Now I am not so good-looking,
I wish I was more attractive,
Oh how I wish.

Charlie Littlewood (8)
New College School

UNDERNEATH THE WAVES

Underneath the waves
Where the water is calm
And where fishes dance and starfish glance
Where the turtles swim
Where shiny fish leap and sing
And where the fast fish zoom
Where the dolphins slap
Where the meat-eaters chase
And people see the beautiful fishes
And flying fishes skim and glide
Where eels slip through the sand
And seaweed is slimy
Where seals splash in the sea
Then they feast and eat
Where the seabed's slippery
And fishes clamp onto the rocks
Where timid fish bounce
Where dangerous sharks eat
And seagulls float on the sea
Then the waves crash on the beach.

Andrew Crawford (8)
New College School

THE SEA'S WORLD

In the sea I saw a little, beautiful fish
It was very shiny and blinding
It was the most beautiful fish I had ever seen

The next day I came back
There was a shoal of fish, they were dancing
And they seemed to be more blinding

The next day I came back, there were five
Jellyfish there

The next day I went diving
I saw a world of fish and blue
As I got deeper and deeper, down and down
There was rubbish
It was all sewage, tar, paint and oil
Which had been dumped there.

Sam Clarke-Warry (9)
New College School

DOLPHINS

I'm a dolphin
We jump up and down in the sea
We sing and dance all day and night
We are darting, feasting, dozing, chasing, splashing in the sea
We're shy, fearful, happy and we don't hurt anyone
We're skidding, gliding through the water
When we sleep we think of good dreams
We hold our breath as we look over the sea
We egg-lay and then they hatch
And we swim beside them, our babies, until they get older
Then we let them go to feed themselves.

Charlie Harnden (9)
New College School

I Seemed To Hang In The Sea Of Blue

The sadness of the sea towers around me,
As I dive under to the deep blue sea.

I see wrecks of old boats,
In the distance I hear a voice,
It says, 'Save us, have mercy!'
As I think, these thoughts come into my mind,
I remember the whale so blue and dark,
The fishes swimming in and out of the weeds,
The sharks and squids eating their prey.
The great shame of the sea comes into my mind,
My thoughts become different,
I despair of the black, sticky oil,
That clings to little fish,
The rubbish that men throw into the water without thinking.

Wouter Vorstman (8)
New College School

Old, Old Lady

Old, old lady
Why do you worry so?
Why do you not come with me and go
To wonderful places
Where we could play with aces
And other game cards?
No more barred doors
Come and talk with us
It's really fun
Let's tell stories of past-times
Until the end of the day.

George Whittow (8)
New College School

A SEA OF JEWELS

The world's most precious gem,
A world of moving gold,
Each piece sparkling
With a shining brilliance,
Their scaled sides
Dappled with shafts of sunlight.

I sit watching each wave break
Thinking of the fishes' kingdom,
The kingdom of laughter and adventure:
Each fish seems to have its story
Each octopus its tale,
They all have their own habits
Each their own ways.

Every fish is the world's wonder
Each one's beauty unmatchable,
The blue whale's spotted side
The killer whale's black patches.

I lie belly down
Looking down on the rocks,
The bare unforgiving rocks.
As I gaze the sea seems to split
As a hundred striped and dappled sides
Pierce a smooth sheet,
Like many stitches on a quilt,
As I walk down the sand path
I watch an angry sea hitting the rocks
As if aiming to squash them to pulp,
Great crested kings, small dribbling servants,
They attack the great barren castle of the rock.
Suddenly I hear a call, unwillingly I turn back.

Alexis Kreager (9)
New College School

THE DEEP OCEAN

In the deep I saw two dolphins
Dipping then diving back into the water again
And crabs and lobsters scuttling
Along the seabed
Whales singing and sharks circling
In the deep
Minute pearls dazzling and glittering
And sparkling
Aren't they amazing on the bottom
Of the deep blue seabed?
Tiny mussels clinging onto seaweed and shells
Uneven starfish and coral reefs
All dotted around the deep seabed
Smooth, wonderful, wet, scaly fish in
Shoals up to seventy
Stinging jellyfish and beautiful sea horses
In the underwater kingdom of the deep
Skimming fish whiz along the surface
Of the water
Slippery, sucking sea anemones on the
Edge of spiky pitch-black rocks
Edgy, cautious fish dart away from predators
Then comes the pollution and destroys many
Living things in the deep of the deep
Shipwrecks all tattered and skeletons and nets
All of those horrible things that pollute
The deep, deep, magnificent sea.

Barnaby McCay (8)
New College School

THE WORLD OF THE BLUE

In the world of the blue below our feet
Where fishes swim and go to sleep
Where happy dolphins dance
And gleeful fishes prance
Where vicious crabs
Give lots of grabs
Where sharks lurk below the
Coral-coated cliffs
Where big, blue whales
Hunt the little plankton
Where turtles glide and swim and dive
Through underwater landscapes
Under our feet is the world of the blue
Full of colourful creatures
So now I know what it's like to be down there
Beneath the coral-coated cliffs.

Otta Jones (9)
New College School

ON THE SEABED

Jumping, rushing, darting, leaping
Into the clear crystal sea
Slippery seals, dancing dolphins
And snapping lobsters
Dazzling, wonderful, smooth

Gleaming coral, glittering sand
Shellfish like the sun, turtles like the clouds
In rushing, salty water
Beneath the rising waves
Wet, scaly, bright, shiny

Enormous whales, tiny eels
Slippery jellyfish, sliding sea lions
Crabs clattering, spiky stingrays
And fierce sharks
Rough, uneven, scratchy and damp
This is what I see drifting through long green weeds.

Thomas Stell (9)
New College School

AGE

As I lie on my sunken feather bed,
I realise a pain,
A pain of age and memory,
I remember what I did and what I had,
But it's gone,
Gone like a shadow,
Like a fire burning out,
I did bloom, I did blossom,
Like the lily buds of May,
But age was winter,
The cold sleet as a sword,
But why am I
What I am and ever forward?
Shadow of death, fetch me,
Oh why? Oh why
Am I left in pain of age and memory?

Robert Brooks (8)
New College School

OLD LADY

Old lady, old lady,
I wonder how you cope to walk
And press the button to cross the road.
Old lady, old lady,
I wish you could be young,
We could run and jump and play.
Old lady, old lady,
Why do you never come out to shop with me?
Old lady, old lady,
Do not be afraid of being mugged.
I will help you to cross the road
And help you to walk.
Do not be scared.
Do not be scared.

Rhys Newcombe-Jones (9)
New College School

UNDER THE DEEP BLUE SEA

I see seaweed hanging from the surface
The water shimmering as the fish swim by
Jellyfish float at the surface
And the stingrays on the sand are zigzagging
I see sea anemones wriggling their way to a cave
In the cave there are black, dangerous rocks
I see shiny wet crabs, lobsters, sharks, octopuses and dolphins
Fly through the waves
I see colourful shells and starfish on the coral reef
The coral reef is dazzling like the sun.

Matthew Thorns (8)
New College School

SCHOOL'S OUT FOR SUMMER

The teacher said, 'Close your books,'
As the children got up with excited looks.
They all rushed out to meet their mums,
Ready to stuff their little tums.
As they run home to jump in the car,
Off they ride over the glistening tar.
Going on their holiday, off to France,
The children's hearts are starting to sing and dance.
We have arrived 'a la maison',
'Quickly get your swimming costume on,
Into the pool, don't be the last,
While the sun's out - it's fading fast.'
Relax, school's over, the fun has begun,
Six weeks of playing and lying in the sun.
'It's good that the summer hols have arrived,
Because I am very tired of work' says Mum.

Natasha Dawe (8)
North Leigh CE Primary School

I HATE SCHOOL

'I'm bored, so bored of school,' I said,
'I'd rather run in the meadows cool,
I'm tired of going in that school hall,
I wish I could swim in a river or pool.

I kind of like English and science,
I'm bored of French and technology,
But break is the best, at least there's no test,
Not to forget maths and biology.'

Katie Halfhead (8)
Rupert House School

TERROR

Terror is tall and thin,
But spends his life
Crouched up in a ball,
So you'll never know,
How big he really is!

His hair is long,
Because he's been hiding
In the cupboard under the stairs
For such a long time
And he's too frightened
To go out to get a haircut!

He's afraid of the dark,
So he has the light on
All day and all night.

He never opens his birthday presents,
Because someone once sent him
A terrifying tarantula
As a joke.

Kate Swann (9)
Rupert House School

TV BROTHER

I wish my brother was a TV,
So I could turn him off!
He has the most disgusting habits
And an annoying cough.

I would be the only one,
The only one in the town,
To have the controls to this TV,
I'd turn his volume down!

I suppose if this did happen,
I'd get bored after a while,
I'd probably wish to turn him back,
Cos he sometimes makes me smile!

Celeste Moberly (10)
Rupert House School

GETTING BETTER

I'm a really rotten reader
I'm the baddest in the class
The sort of rotten reader
That makes the others laugh

I'm a really awful writer
I make an awful mess
I end up with the ink
Splattered on my desk

I'm a really dreadful speller
And I find it hard to add
And science is confusing
It really is too bad!

I cannot paint in art
I cannot draw a yard
I cannot throw a ball
And hockey is too hard

I really try my hardest
I hope you understand
I know one day that I'll improve
I'll be the best in all the land.

Sophia Lerche-Thomsen (8)
Rupert House School

THE UPPER SCHOOL DISCO

Today is the upper school disco,
Everyone's bouncing with joy.
Rachel and Mick we caught kissing,
He's such a popular boy!

Annie is doing her make-up,
Slapping on blusher and cream.
Nattie's got millions to choose from,
Jessie has stopped being mean!

The teachers are all looking glamorous,
Dressed up in boob tubes and all!
We're dancing upon the tables,
Everyone's having a ball!

We're all getting double excited,
My bra nearly fell to my feet!
The principal danced his old head off,
No one stayed put in their seat!

Katherine Innes (10)
Rupert House School

UNDER THE SEA

Under the sea where dolphins play,
Fish dart and starfish sway,
But deeper down on the dark sea floor,
Strange things are lurking, more and more,
Blue flashing lights and big bulging eyes,
Huge clashing fangs of a fish in disguise,
Then there is darkness, nothing to see,
On the bottom of the deep blue sea.

Annie Moberly (8)
Rupert House School

THE HIPPY HAMSTER

My hamster's really hippy
Her teeth are really nippy
Her eyes very bright
When she gets up at night

My hamster's really sweet
She has really little feet
Her whiskers are all twitchy
Her nose is really titchy

My hamster's really cute
Her teeth are so minute
Her nose is really small
It's hardly there at all

My hamster's really nosy
Her little ears are really rosy
She's got really cuddly fur
And I think the world of her.

Hannah Baker (8)
Rupert House School

UNDER THE SEA

Over the waves where the sea is blue,
The white horses dance and as they do,
The dolphins jump up two by two
And the starfish are quiet as they creep through,
The forest of seaweed which slowly grew,
On the rocks where only a few
Oysters sleep in their beds of goo!

Ella Shepard (8)
Rupert House School

GOLDEN SUNSETS

Golden glitters the dew on the leaves,
Golden corn in the golden sheaves,
Golden mice in the golden sun,
Golden sky when day is done.

Golden flowers in the golden beds,
Golden hens in the golden sheds,
Golden flies in the golden air,
Golden sun on my golden hair.

Golden fields ripple in the breeze,
Golden fruit hangs from golden trees,
Golden clouds drift in the skies,
Golden sun sets and dies.

Camilla Hopkinson (8)
Rupert House School

MY FLOWER

I have a magical flower,
She shines her petals at me.
She slowly sways her head,
She's as lovely as can be.

Now it's nearly spring,
Her petals open wide.
She has a drop of nectar,
Hidden deep inside.

She is a brilliant blue,
With petals layer on layer.
She sits on my window sill
And her perfume fills the air.

Amira Burshan (8)
Rupert House School

SWEETS

A Polo is a tasty sweet
Which people like me like to eat
Maltesers are round and they crunch
When you eat them after lunch

Starbursts are nice and chewy
When you eat them they go gooey!
Milky Bars are flat and white
I save them up to eat at night

Curly Wurlys twist and twirl
They are like plaits upon a girl
I think that nothing beats
A great big bag of lovely sweets!

Arabella Boardman (8)
Rupert House School

UNDER THE SEA

Dolphins curve their backs.
Sea anemones open
like buds bursting.
Sea horses jig past
like hiccupping bones.
Stingrays glide
like silent spaceships.
Crabs scuttle around
like mechanical spiders.
Jellyfish dance
like swaying cling film.
Starfish wander
like sluggish hands.

Laura Wheatley (9)
Rupert House School

My Pet From Mars

My pet is really unusual
I bought it when I was on Mars
He is like a blob of green jelly
His eyes twinkle like stars

His hair is dyed bright-purple
It sticks right up on end
His nose is shaped like a pear
He's completely round the bend!

His legs are bendy like rubber
His arms stick out like a twig
He likes to play in the garden
Because he loves to dig

He talks a load of rubbish
He's hard to understand
But although he's really unusual
He's the best pet in the land!

Sophie McDowell (9)
Rupert House School

Keeping Watch

I am a meerkat
Standing like a sentry
Watching for lions
Keep away! No entry!

I'm on the lookout
For eagles up high
For we are their prey
And we don't want to die!

At the top of a tree
I watch for a snake
Slithering towards me
I must keep awake!

I am a meerkat
I give the alarm
To the rest of the pack
To keep them from harm.

Rosie Thake (8)
Rupert House School

THE CHEATING CHEETAH

I am a cheetah
And I cheat at cards,
So beware if you play me,
To beat me is hard!

I am a cheetah,
I cheat day and night,
I cheat all the lions,
It gives them a fright.

I am a cheetah
I cheat day and night,
I cheat all the lions,
It gives them a fright.

I am a cheetah,
I cheat night and day,
I make sure I win,
So they have to pay.

Victoria Bushnell (8)
Rupert House School

BREAK

Tick-tock! Watching the clock,
Waiting to go out to break,
This class is so dull and quiet,
How will I stay awake?

Ding-dong! Goes the bell,
At last the lesson ends!
I grab my crisps and coat
And run out to my friend's!

We play catch and skipping
And every sort of game.
Today it's our turn,
On the climbing frame.

Ding-dong! Goes the bell
And back inside we troop,
It's another tiring lesson
And our heads begin to droop.

Alice Buys (8)
Rupert House School

HEDGEHOGS

Nobody seems to like hedgehogs much,
I don't think it's very fair,
I know why people don't like them,
It's because they don't have hair!

They do have spiky prickles,
That look sharp and tough,
But inside them is an animal,
That isn't at all rough.

Promise me that next time
You meet a little one,
You'll speak to it quite gently,
So it does not run.

Penny Hall (8)
Rupert House School

THE BURGLAR

The owls are hooting in the dark, black night,
Cats outside begin to fight,
I looked outside and on turned the light,
A burglar tiptoed through the night!

Downstairs I heard a big bang,
It sounded like the heavens rang,
I quietly tiptoed out of bed,
'I'm going downstairs,' I bravely said.

Downstairs I tiptoed past the creaky stair
And you'll never guess who I saw down there?
A burglar stealing silver and gold
And other things that could be sold!

All at once I gave a shout,
The burglar jumped and ran straight out!
He ran into a man in blue
''Ello, 'ello, 'ello, I know you!'

The burglar then began to wail,
As he was taken straight to jail.
So now I can sleep safe and sound
And not wake up until morning comes round.

Olivia Barton (9)
Rupert House School

ANGER

Anger is a wild man!
He is terrible!
He has a stallion
And a bloodstained sword.
He has one red eye
And a big hooked nose.
His ears are small and mean
And his mouth is a white line.
Most of his hair has been torn out,
But what is left is wild and matted.

He does not wash,
He lives in a deserted place
And his head is filled with how to kill!

Alexandra Boardman (10)
Rupert House School

ANGER

Anger has the wildest hair
He's got black beady eyes and a furious stare!

He wears a long black tattered coat
And has barbed wire around his throat!

He has a snarling sharp-toothed grin,
When he gets drunk from too much gin!

His toenails have ripped through his slippers,
They make his toes look like big nippers.

You might think his head is going to pop,
'Cause when he swells he cannot stop!

Alexandra Barbour (10)
Rupert House School

TERROR

Terror is a thin, bony man,
He wears narrow shoes
And his hair stands on end.
He wears a white feather coat,
With yellow clothes underneath.
He has goose bumps all over his skin,
Which is pale and cold.
His eyes are huge and staring,
As they dart all over the place.
His yellow teeth chatter
And he jumps in alarm.
He mumbles nervously,
But every now and then he suddenly
Screams!

Lisa Szego (9)
Rupert House School

GREED

Greed is a bloated king!
He is a horrible, childish, middle-aged man.
He looks like Henry VIII.
He is an only child and a mummy's boy!
He *never* has enough money,
Even though he is buried in gold!

He has a bad attitude
And yells, 'I want that!'
He makes sure he gets it!

He never shares and has no friends,
(Except for Jealousy and Impatience.)

Amelia Thornton (9)
Rupert House School

Terror

Terror is a harvest mouse,
Who is lost in the City of Cats!
He shivers and shakes
And hides in a tiny hole.
He is very thin
And he is starving,
His clothes are tattered.

He is a pale-brown
And he has long thin whiskers.
He rubs his face
With his tiny paws
And he nibbles his nails.

His eyes are black beads,
He lives on chewed-up cardboard
And drinks drain water.

Alicia Holder (10)
Rupert House School

Love

Love is a fluffy, winged angel,
Who flies to and fro.
Her Cupid's bow and arrow,
She is shooting down below.

She wears a lovely dress,
With a glittering diamond heart.
She's carried by two silver horses,
Who pull her golden cart.

Her hair is long and golden,
Her eyes are big and blue.
Her lips are soft and baby-pink,
She's always good and true.

Georgie Griffiths (9)
Rupert House School

FRIENDSHIP

Friendship has rosy-red cheeks,
Warm eyes and a massive smile.
She skips along the street,
With her friend, Comradeship.
They will always be friends.

Friendship lives in a world of paradise,
With her friends alongside her,
Talking and giggling, waving and smiling.

Friendship gallops along the beach,
Splashing in the waves
And having a good time.

Friendship wears pink shorts
And a frilly white top.
She eats ice cream, but whenever she eats,
She gives some to her friends.

Friendship shares everything
And nothing is told to one person and not the other.
Friendship and Comradeship will always be together,
When they visit the City of Adversity.

Charly Binney (10)
Rupert House School

CAKES AND SWEETS

Cakes and sweets,
Fab sticky eats,
Far better than vegetables
And meats.

Rising in the oven,
They taste great,
I love sweets
And gorgeous cakes.

Like chocolate, toffee
And caramel,
Rolled into one,
The hot cakes will always sell.

All cream and chocolate,
Oh, so yummy,
I take big bites,
Cos they're scrummy.

So at the end,
They're the best eats,
I have to have
Those cakes and sweets!

Tuula Costelloe (10)
Rupert House School

THE MERMAID'S ADVENTURE

The mermaids wake up from their sleep
They want to swim down to the deep
With flowing tails they dive below
To where sea monsters shine and glow

They see weird faces in the dark
And then they meet a great big shark!
They all go *'Arhh!'* and swim away
Back to the safety of the bay!

Georgina Williams-Gray (8)
Rupert House School

FAITH

Faith is a young girl,
Her hair is straight, blonde and tidy.
Her eyes are a strong blue,
She is always smiling,
To inspire other people.

She rides a strong, sleek white horse
And wears a spotless, pure-white dress,
She is never ill! She never falters.

Her hair blows back from her glowing face,
When she rides her trusty steed.
She wears the Ring of Belief
And the Necklace of the Good.
She hangs out in Heaven,
With Hope and Love,
For they are the messengers
Of the Lord.

When she has been through
A wood or the meadows,
The leaves and the grass
Whisper her name -
Faith.

Emma Collinson (10)
Rupert House School

Fury

Fury is the knight,
With blood dripping down
His scarred face,
Which is crisscrossed with stitches!
His dirty armour gleams.
He has pointed black and yellow teeth,
Which snarl through his dirty beard.
His eyes are bully's eyes,
Beady and cruel.
He smells like rotten fish.
He rides a wild horse,
Covered in bruises and whip marks.
He beats his wife,
Whenever she does something wrong!

***Katherine Poulter (10)**
Rupert House School*

Suffering

Suffering is an old wizened lady,
Bed-bound and wrapped in white blankets.
She is in awful pain!
You can see it in her eyes,
You can see all her ribs,
Because she eats so little.
Her mouth is dry
And she is always thirsty.

Suffering lives all over the world,
In the home of ordinary people,
But her friends are Hope, Faith and Kindness
And they are always with her.

***Emily Granger (10)**
Rupert House School*

HARRY POTTER

Harry Potter, a wizard,
He has sticking-up, black, messy hair.
He's got a jaggedy scar on his forehead,
Which You-Know-Who once put there.

He's got an owl called Hedwig,
Her feathers are fluffy and white.
She delivers his parcels and letters
And flies through the dark, velvet night.

He lives with the horrible Dursleys,
Who are scared of his magical powers.
In the cupboard, under the stairs,
He's locked up for hours and hours.

He goes to a school called Hogwarts,
Where Albus Dumbledore's Head.
Ron and Hermione like him,
But Malfoy'd prefer he was dead!

He learns about witches and wizards
And brews up interesting spells,
But sometimes when Snape's teaching potions,
He creates some horrible smells!

Harry is Seeker in Quidditch,
He rides around on a broom.
The Golden Snitch is elusive,
But the Nimbus 2000 goes zoom!

Harry's quite fond of Hagrid,
Who likes monstrous beasts.
They dine in a magical hall,
Where they have some magnificent feasts!

Ruth Collins (9)
Rupert House School

FAITH

Faith is a white Shetland pony,
With a strong mane and tail.

Faith's coat is glossy,
She believes in herself.

She lives free on the hill,
Believing in anything she wants.

Faith trusts in her mother, Hope,
Who is a beautiful light mare.

Faith stands on the crest of the hill,
Gazing at the wonders of the world.

Faith relies on herself alone
And canters on shiny hooves.

Faith knows no boundaries
And lives forever.

Emily Binning (10)
Rupert House School

GENEROSITY

Generosity looks like a fluffy, turquoise-blue,
It smells like little buds blossoming,
Generosity tastes sweet and juicy,
It feels soft and smooth,
It sounds like children laughing,
Generosity lives in the depths
Of
My
Heart.

Adam Lubbock (10)
St Laurence CE Primary School, Warborough

THE MAGIC BOX

I will put in the box
A flitter from the flap of a flying carpet
A flame from the first Indian
And the last breath of a prancing deer
I will put in the box
The trickling ripples from a calm stream
And the dawning of a blue sun
I will put in the box
The silky swish from three golden wishes
The broken heart of a baby
And the love of a mother
I will put in the box
Five vibrant petals
Six winter breezes on a cloudy day
And the pant of a golden dog after a day's walk in a forest of fire

My box is fashioned with ice like silver and rays from the sun
Like glistening jewels and gold.

I shall bathe in the sea with rippling waves
With the sun high above
And the beach of golden pebbles washed beneath my feet.

Samantha Alfred (100
St Laurence CE Primary School, Warborough

POWER

Power is sea blue
It smells like strong perfume
Power tastes like sharp metal
It sounds like crashing water
It feels tough and strong
Power lies in a heart.

Richard Meadows (9)
St Laurence CE Primary School, Warborough

THE MAGIC BOX

I will put in this box
A butterfly with golden wings glinting in the sun
A flower with peach yellow petals as beautiful as the world

I will put in the box
A child's laughter on a spring morning
A pint of water from Nevada falls
A sigh from a tree with the breezy wind

I will put in the box
Dew on a winter morning
A robin fluttering from tree to tree
Sand from the Sahara Desert

I will put in the box
A piranha from an Indian beach
A music box with children singing
A brick from Atlantis, mouldy green

I will put in the box
A sixth sense, the sense of magic
Memories of my life
50% of all the knowledge in the world

My box is carved from molten lava
Filled with a wealth that could not be guessed
And with the hinges of time opening every Millennium

In my box I will never be lonely for I have all my animal friends
And my summer vacation in my pocket
And all the laughter in the world in my heart.

Callum McLarty (9)
St Laurence CE Primary School, Warborough

THE MAGIC BOX

I will put in the box
A herd of leaping gazelles charging through the desert,
Pollen from blooming flowers, colourful and bright,
The spark from a shooting star shining through the night.

I will put in the box
Two magic monsters all fluffy and blue,
The stripes from a terrified zebra leaping ever so high
And a golden key with no magical lock to fit in.

I will put in the box
The hands of a ticking clock with new numbers to match,
A swarm of buzzing bees hovering over sweet nectar,
A scale from a slimy fish all green and sparkling.

I will put in the box
Nine colours of the night sky on a summer's day,
The hair from a lion's tail like a golden strand of thread,
A leaf from the oldest tree fluttering down to the ground.

My box is made of grass all fresh and green,
With rose petals inside smelling as sweet as candyfloss,
Its hinges are made of daisy stems and shiny green leaves.

I shall enter my box, fall on a heap of soft feathers,
All white just like snow,
Wake up feeling happy, sit on a soft, warm rug,
Right next to an orange fire flickering so bright,
Almost like a mini sun, a fireball,
Such a beautiful sight.

Jodie Stanley (10)
St Laurence CE Primary School, Warborough

THE MAGIC BOX

I will put in my box
A summer day with the cool breeze blowing through the trees,
The sun and moon glowing with joy,
My best climbing tree with squirrels dancing.

I will put in my box
The 39th hour of the 39th day of the 39th month,
The candyfloss clouds swimming in the air,
The seas of St Lucia with boats on the horizon.

I will put in my box
The flowers' smile as the bees spread pollen,
The gleeful shouts of joy from children playing,
The key of life turning in its lock.

My box is fashioned with pearls of hope,
Shimmering in the sunset,
With evergreen trees with their secrets hidden,
Silver dragons bursting with golden fire.

I shall fly in my box
And find huge mountains to climb,
All the mountains I shall climb,
I will put up a flag of freedom.

Patrick Rider (11)
St Laurence CE Primary School, Warborough

The Magic Box

I will put in the box
A magic carpet to take me anywhere
A bird that can fly faster than the speed of light
A cloud made out of candyfloss

I will put in the box
A giant ladybird attacking a cheetah
A house made out of a burger
A shop with everything in it

I will put in the box
A door that leads to another world
A fist as hard as volcanic rock
A moon as gold as a crown

I will put in my box
Some wool from a sheep
A seed blowing in the wind
A snail struggling out of its shell

My box is made out of old bones
The hinges are like when you move
When you open it you feel happy

I shall grind down the stairs like Tony Hawk
And fall in a bundle of soft pillows.

Daniel Haynes (10)
St Laurence CE Primary School, Warborough

THE MAGIC BOX

I will put in the box
The sound of trickling water from a stream,
The first flower with yellow petals as bright and colourful as the sun,
A child's playful laugh at Christmas.

I will put in the box
The sound of dropping golden coins,
A silky kitten playing with cotton wool,
A spider's shimmering web on a frosty winter's morning.

I will put in the box
The first sparkling star of a black deserted night,
A fluttering golden butterfly
And a mother caring for her baby.

I will put in the box
A witch with a magic lamp and a genie on a broomstick
And a silver sea.

My box has gold and silver stars on it
And butterflies in the corners,
Its lock is made of ice.

I shall skate in my box on curving paths
And stop in a pure green countryside park.

Sara Bailey (10)
St Laurence CE Primary School, Warborough

THE MAGIC BOX

I will put in my magic box
A fluffy white cloud on a summer's day
The silk inside a chestnut shell
The smell of perfumed lavender

I will put in my magic box
The bluest water on the shore
The fin of a fish splashing
The splash of a dolphin diving into water

I will put in my magic box
The flicker of light from a candle
The sound of children playing
The echo of church bells ringing

I will put in my magic box
A farmer riding a black horse
And a horse rider in a tractor cab
A night with a light sky

My box is carved with ancient writing
And the first family's picture on it
The first hoof of a white horse

I will ice skate in my box on an ice skating rink
I will swim in my box in the bluest seas.

Emily Cox (10)
St Laurence CE Primary School, Warborough

THE MAGIC BOX

I will put in the box
The summer's gloomy night with birds swooping around,
A web from a spider's shimmering silk,
A razor sharp spine from a hedgehog's naily back.

I will put in the box
The warm breath of a newborn silky dog,
A cup of sticky oil from under the wavy sea,
A barn mouse's fluff that's all golden and tangled.

I will put in the box
A scaly snake skin that's just been shed,
The last breath of a sea lion's life,
A part of a boat that has sailed round the world.

I will put in the box
A summer's shiny day,
A fiery dragon's scaly back
And a snowman with a carrot nose

My box is as ice-cold shiny steel,
With a picture of a sea sweeping up all the rocks,
Its huge pencil hinges help it stay supported.

I shall skate on ramps,
As high as a house,
On the biggest skate-park,
Then I'll get flipped to a beach
That is the colour of the orange sun.

Christopher Blevins (11)
St Laurence CE Primary School, Warborough

THE MAGIC BOX

I will put in the box
Three delicate wishes from across the seas
A gentle tidal wave from South America
A steady breeze like a smooth sea

I will put in the box
A silk smooth cloud from a winter's day
A town of fairies and goblins with little green hats
A dragon with a foggy fiery breath

I will put in the box
A moon with silver-frosted rings
A silken feather from a golden eagle
Some sparkly dust from a silver moon

I will put in the box
A cloudless sky with a bright yellow sunset
A frosty winter's day
And a warm summer's night

My box is designed with stars, suns and moons on the lid
Blue wishes in the corners
And is made from the leaves from an autumn day

I shall swim with dolphins and whales
In a calm sea just off the coast of Spain
Then they take me down to the bottom of the sea
And I shall see
Baby dolphins and whales.

Bethan Curl (9)
St Laurence CE Primary School, Warborough

THE MAGIC BOX

I will put in my box
The juice from a sweet scarlet raspberry,
A snowball-white rabbit bouncing down the deepest hole,
Five silky, bright flower petals shining in the sun.

I will put in my box,
The sparkling rings from the planet Saturn,
A chilly breeze from Pluto,
The big red spot from Jupiter.

I will put in my box,
The last icicle from a frozen winter,
A bright orange carrot from a snowman,
A frozen white snowball.

I will put in my box,
A golden strand of a lion's mane,
A princess in the sea
And a whale in a castle.

My box is fashioned from coloured pencil lead and snow,
With rubber stars and diamonds,
Its hinges are made from dog claws.

I shall swim with dolphins in my box,
In the seas of America,
Then go down to the bottom of the sea and meet exotic fish.

Rebecca Emerson (10)
St Laurence CE Primary School, Warborough

The Magic Box

I will put in the box
The petal of a red, red rose when blossomed.
The chatter of children at break time, playing.
The stillness of a tiled roof when the winter comes.

I will put in the box
The wonders of the underwater world,
Fish to fish to fish.
A conker dropping from a tree.
The cackle of a witch's laugh when evil comes her way.

I will put in the box
A secret passed from friend to friend.
An old man with a walking stick, on a summer's day.
A ballerina on her toes, dancing the night away.

I will put in the box
The lick of a tall, tall tree, while a dog is flowering leaves.
The green, green sky shining on the blue meadow on a bright day.
The seed flowering in the ground and the flower growing roots.

My box is fashioned by a ghostly-white,
But the outside does not count, for open the lid and . . .
Away!

I shall ride in the box on my fantasy horse
And win races that come my way
And end on a beach with silky sand and waves lapping over the shore.
The sun will go down, the green sky go black
And I'll sleep the night away!

Mollie Hodge (10)
St Laurence CE Primary School, Warborough

Magic Box

I will put in my box
A flying fish with 20 wings,
A sheep with a neck of 100 metres,
A mushroom forest with tiny goblins.

I will put in my box
A magic map that will tell you anything,
A cursed zombie roaming around his grave,
A tree that has springs for a trunk.

I will put in my box
A giant mouse with teeth bigger than a wardrobe,
An elephant sized 1cm,
A red dragon breathing ice.

I will put in my box
A tidal wave with surfing mummies,
A land of candy with chocolate rivers,
A wonderland with
Everything you ever need.

My box is fashioned with jewels of hope
And tiny pearls that sparkle in the summer's sun,
Beauty that cannot be described
And somewhere, somehow,
There is a beautiful, shimmering shell.

Inside my box,
I shall fly over the diamond trees
And admire the wonderland of dreams,
There I will have all my dreams and better,
I will rocket over thorny plains
And fly over streams,
All you ever want is in my box . . . and beyond.

Oliver Picken (10)
St Laurence CE Primary School, Warborough

DEATH

Death is black
It smells like a dead carcass
Death tastes like a cup of blood
It sounds like someone in pain and agony
It feels like a skull
Death lives in the middle of a battlefield.

Michael Gibbons (10)
St Laurence CE Primary School, Warborough

DOLPHIN

Merry mammal,
Pod member,
Excellent swimmer,
Wave surfer,
Noisy talker,
Lively leaper,
Fantastic acrobat,
High jumper,
Graceful glider,
Fast skimmer,
Clever buddy,
Smiling face,
Sea creature,
Ocean entertainer,
Friendly mate!

Harriet Kitching (10)
St Mary's School, Henley-On-Thames

The Wild Waterfall

The wild waterfall,
Discovered in the mountains,
Rapid, gushing, fierce,
Like a bird diving for its prey,
Like a dolphin leaping over the waves,
Makes me feel nervous,
Like a daffodil about to be picked,
The wild waterfall,
Reminds me how beautiful nature is.

Antonia Barker (10)
St Mary's School, Henley-On-Thames

Waterfall

Calm, peaceful, flowing.
Power growing.
Racing, rippling water.
Fast, furious rapids.
Razor, rigid rocks.
Endless, timeless drop.
Crashing, thunderous froth.
White, misty spray.
Calm water again.

Henry Svendsen (10)
St Mary's School, Henley-On-Thames

The Tiger

A fierce fighter
A hungry hunter
A sneaky stalker
A glaring eye
A razor tooth
A claw of daggers

A stare of steel
A striding stripe
A deadly kill
A fatal predator
An elegant beast
An orange striped carnivore!

Charles Kronsten (10)
St Mary's School, Henley-On-Thames

THE HUGE MOUNTAIN

The huge mountain
Sixteen times taller than the tallest tower
Great, mighty, strong
Like a pyramid growing and growing
Like a house with lots of rooms
It makes me want to be the first one to climb it
Like a great hero the huge mountain
Reminds us that we can't be the tallest in the world.

Natalie Bishop (10)
St Mary's School, Henley-On-Thames

THE APPLE

The apple,
A sweet fruit that grows on trees,
Round, juicy, green,
Like a green ball rolling towards me,
Like a meal in itself,
It makes me feel huge,
Like the sky watching over us,
The apple,
Reminds us how sweet things can be.

Elizabeth Walton (10)
St Mary's School, Henley-On-Thames

IN THE DARK

There were faces on my curtains
A monstrous creature in the corner

A hand reaching from my desk

Someone is wearing my kilt
Red blood dripping down my wall
A deadly smell

Something monstrous is in my bed
Spooky shadows reflecting from my mirror

Doors slam shut
Someone is talking.

Fiona Stewart (9)
St Mary's School, Henley-On-Thames

DARKNESS

Darkness creeping up behind you
Making you shiver with fright
You hear spooky sounds calling you
Calling you
From the mist
The curtains twist and turn
Making ghost-like figures
To pull you to your death
The floor creaks as someone's trying to get you
What was that
In the window?
Cackling!

Matthew Stewart (11)
St Mary's School, Henley-On-Thames

THE NIGHT STEALER

Shadows, noises, fear and sights, touch and smell and horror and frights

This is the mixture of the night stealer
His master is the shadow creeper

He creeps around your house at night
He wakes you up and gives you a fright

His worst enemy is the power of light
Which drives him back into the depths of night

His cloak is shadow, his crown is fear
In his hand he holds; screams, howls and bad dreams
When dawn comes it drives him back into the light and into the day.

Guy Pawson (11)
St Mary's School, Henley-On-Thames

THE GIANT OAK

The giant oak,
Hundreds of years old,
Glorious, luscious, enduring,
Like a magnificent eagle braced for flight,
Like a benign giant with arms outstretched.

It makes me feel secure,
Like a sleeping child safe in its mother's arms,
The giant oak,
Reminds me of the past and all the things that the giant oak
Has seen before my time.

Ella May James (10)
St Mary's School, Henley-On-Thames

THE WOODS

A green mass
A brown hollow
A creature's Heaven
A city man's sorrow

A bird's choir
A hunting season
A walker's dream
A paradise

A green mass
A brown hollow
A creature's Heaven
An animal's home.

Hannah Nugent (10)
St Mary's School, Henley-On-Thames

THE HUGE TIDAL WAVE

The huge tidal wave,
As big as a tower,
Gigantic, invincible, unbeatable,
Like a knife cutting things in its way,
Like the Great Wall of China made from water,
Makes me feel like a scaredy-cat,
Like a mouse born to make fun of,
The huge tidal wave,
Try to love the sea before it's too late.

Etienne Bataille (10)
St Mary's School, Henley-On-Thames

THE BIKER

The wind was a torrent of darkness among the gusty trees,
The moon was a ghostly car light shining through the misty sky,
The road was a ribbon of moonlight over the purple moor
And the biker came revving, revving - revving up to the nightclub door.
He had a jet-black helmet on his forehead with his visor down to
                                                                    his chin,
A jacket of the darkest and finest leather
And trousers of denim blue.
They fitted without a wrinkle,
His boots came up to his knees.
He rode with his tyres burning,
His pistol barrels burning,
His knuckledusters shining under the deep, dark sky.
Over granite he rode with rocks flying in the nightclub park,
He tapped his whip on the back door, but everything was locked and guarded.
He whistled a tune and who should be waiting but . . .
The club owners black-eyed daughter.

Robert Alderman (11)
Thomas Reade Primary School

THE DUCK

I can catch fish with great succeed
And uproot all the pond's weed
I can dive right down in the river
Or if I climb out, it'll make me shiver
Bread I can eat and take off to the south
I can attack at my foe with my mouth
When I have ducklings, I'll show them around
And order them to trample the mounds.

Nicholas Mould (9)
Thomas Reade Primary School

RAIN

I can water the land when the ground starts to crack
And the gaps start to fill as I cry my damp tears
I can banish the sun as my teardrops fall down
Or as the sun sleeps, I start slowly to creep

As I drizzle and start to pow
I have all night to do what I want
And if the sun starts to shine
There will be a rainbow
And my tears drip down the window
As I start to rain

I am in the sky and when I fall I can turn to ice
When I hit the ground, I rebound and go back up again
I can come with thunder
I can come with lightning

I can flood very fast
When I run through the streets
I can water the flowers
I can dance on puddles, ponds and rivers.

Christopher Eccles (10)
Thomas Reade Primary School

THE LION

I can run and walk and bound
And fight with my friends on hot summer days
I can jump and leap and cry
Or kill a bird without any knife
And run across fields and catch fish in the lake
But when I am spent, I lie still and quiet.

Katherine Hudson (10)
Thomas Reade Primary School

THE WIND

When the wind is howling between the buildings
It is a dolphin humming to its friends

When the wind is whispering through the trees
It is a cheetah trying to arrest its prey

When the wind is making a cold draught through the house
It is a polar bear wandering around and around in some sort of
                                                                              time zone

When the wind is flicking flames in a fire
It is a dragon trying to prepare its dinner

When the wind is blowing an umbrella inside out
It is a ghost creeping up upon someone and . . . ahh!

When the wind is breaking branches off a tree
It is a stampede of elephants running away from poachers.

Lucy White (11)
Thomas Reade Primary School

TWISTER

I can lift off a roof and not use a crane,
Wrestle with water and chuck it around,
I will pull out the grass and blow it away
And take all the leaves and spin them around.
Pull the trees from all of the ground,
I will knock all the houses from off of the their perch,
I will smash all the windows with only a touch,
But when I am done, I would not hurt a fly.

Thomas Turner (10)
Thomas Reade Primary School

THE WIND

When the wind is howling between the buildings,
It is a pack of dogs speeding after a fox.

When the wind is whispering through the trees,
It is a spider revolving its silver web.

When the wind is making a cold draught in the house,
It is a ghost hurtling from one room to another.

When the wind is flickering flames in a fire,
It is a dragon baking its delicious dinner.

When the wind is blowing umbrellas inside out,
It is a mischievous imp playing naughty tricks.

When the wind is breaking branches off a tree,
It is a rhino walking slowly towards its banquet.

Stephanie Gerring (11)
Thomas Reade Primary School

THE BACKSTREET THUG

The wind was a torrent of darkness among the gusty trees,
The moon was a scary speedboat tossed upon cloudy seas.
The road was a slithering serpent between the city's shops
And the backstreet thug came zooming - zooming - zooming.
The backstreet thug came zooming up to the pub he bopped.

He's a baseball cap on his forehead, a collar of spikes round his neck,
A jacket of skin-tight leather and jeans which were a wreck.
They fitted incredibly tightly, his boots made his mother sigh
And he zoomed with a smoking exhaust pipe, his cigarette
                                              butts all alight.
His studded belt looked a fright, under the night sky.

Lucy Killoran & Sarah Woolhouse (11)
Thomas Reade Primary School

A Parody Of A Parody Of Hiawatha

In the nursery garden playing,
Children heard the teacher saying,
Naughty, naughty you'll get caughty,
No I won't but you are forty!
Snack time now, it's time for eating,
Lots of children crying, weeping,
Juice and biscuits, yummy, yummy,
Infants shouting, 'Mummy, Mummy.'
Something wet inside his nappy,
He does not look very happy,
Mummy come, say hello Tony,
Daddy's waiting on the phony.
Tony angry, smash up mobile,
Screams, 'Mummy crazy she go wild.'

Natalie O'Hare (10)
Thomas Reade Primary School

The Wind

When the wind is howling between buildings,
It is wolf desperately trying to find its lost cubs.
When the wind is whispering through the trees,
It is a tiger soundlessly hunting.
When the wind is making a cold draught in the house,
It is a penguin looking for its friends.
When the wind is flicking flames in a fire,
It is a dragon defending its gold.
When the wind is blowing umbrellas inside-out,
It is a ghost frightfully haunting.
When the wind is breaking branches off a tree,
It is a destroyer.

Zoe Graubner (9)
Thomas Reade Primary School

A Parody Of A Parody Of Hiawatha!

By the snack timetable dribbling,
Sat a crazy watching sibling!
Playing games with little dollies,
Licking, slurping on their lollies!
Screaming, shouting, laughing, weeping,
One small boy was only sleeping!
'Time to go now, come with Mummy.'
'No! No! No! I've dropped my dummy!'
'Da dummy's lost, oh where is it?
Now I know, it's in the sandpit!'
'No, no, no, please let me stay.'
'No, we'll come back another day!'
So now the playing children go,
Except just one who hurt his toe!

Rose Gallagher (10)
Thomas Reade Primary School

The Sea

The sea is a fearsome lion,
It leaps and pounces on the heaving waves,
It shakes its great shaggy mane,
Over the horror-stricken rocks.

When it is thirsty, it roars at the remorseless sky
And laps ferociously at the raging storm.

Then it finally lays down its great golden mane,
On the vast, gilded sand.
Taking no notice as the circling water crowds around him.

Susan Shi (10)
Thomas Reade Primary School

THE SEED

I am an immortal hitch-hiker
I climb on you when you don't see me
You do not see me, microscopic, a pin point end
So small, so tiny

A warrior as strong as gold
I can defeat any seed, even one the size
Of a ball, will tangle it then to a mole

The only thing I don't dare defeat
Is a human and an animal
My only weak spot which does then kill me
That gives me a lot of pain and anger
And that thing only a human can control
No sun and water, will then kill me.

Matthew Wilson (9)
Thomas Reade Primary School

SEA PREDATOR

The sea lion charges at the shore,
Waving his shaggy mane, he roars,
The roar echoes around the rocks,
Giving people an almighty shock,
He waves his mane as he reaches the land,
Making them spread out on the sand.

In summer when the wind has gone,
The lion lies, asleep at dawn,
The sun shines down upon the sea,
A golden coal shining brilliantly,
Until he awakes and brings much fear.

Alastair Gregory (10)
Thomas Reade Primary School

MOUSETRAP

Cat is hungry, cat is hungry,
'Time for dinner' he said,
There is a mouse living in a hole
And soon he will be dead,
Off goes the hungry cat,
To go and catch his prey,
I'll have to find him first
And soon he will be dead.

The very hungry cat,
Saw the mouse in a hat,
He went to go and kill him,
But the mouse had ran away,
The cat was nearly crying,
Because the mouse was not dying,
The mouse was nearly flying,
I'll have to find him again
And soon he will be dead.

The cat goes off again,
He goes to find the mouse,
He needs to have his dinner,
Hungry and thirsty,
The cat runs up the stairs,
He wasn't playing dares,
Into the room with the mouse,
I'll have to find him now.

The cat was very drowsy,
The mouse was in his hole,
The cat went to eat his cat food
And the mouse said, 'Phew'.

Naomi Keating (10)
Thomas Reade Primary School

THE ATTACK OF THE DOLPHINS

Swim to catch them, swim to catch them,
Swim to catch them dolphins.
Down in the dark, deep, deep water,
Swam the school of dolphins.
We have to swim along,
Raise the fish to the surface.
Into a storm of salmon,
Swam the school of dolphins.

We have to swim along,
Was there a dolphin left behind?
Not the calf knew,
The fish were terrified.
The dolphins were swimming,
The water was dimming.
The fish were aiming,
Into a storm of salmon,
Swam the school of dolphins.

Fish to the right of them,
Fish to the left of them,
Fish in front of them,
Swim and eat.
Swirl with flip and swish,
Proudly swam towards the fish,
Into the jaws of death.
Into the moment of floating,
Swam the school of dolphins.

When will their glory fade?
Oh, the wild swim they made!
Honour the dolphin brigade,
Swam the school of dolphins.

Hannah Burfitt (11)
Thomas Reade Primary School

Rain

I can water the land when the ground starts to crack
And the gaps start to fill as I cry my damp tears

I can banish the sun as my teardrops fall down
Or as the sun sleeps, start slowly to creep

I can creep from the sun without it noticing me
And trickle down from the windows, I can make people really wet

I can make ducks really happy with my wetness from the rain
Or I turn to ice when I'm cold and people can ice skate on me

I can grow lots of flowers when people put bulbs into the ground
And flood cities and towns when the sun isn't looking

I can make people have colds with my wetness
Or when the sun comes out, that is the end of me!

Dara Probets (10)
Thomas Reade Primary School

The Snow

I can make you feel cold like an ice cube,
And leave you in a coat of snow.
I can perform a whirlwind,
Or create a furious blizzard.
Trees I can freeze and also their roots,
I can frost the leaves and cover them in diamonds.
When I pass by I freeze the ground,
And leave you with white frost.

Bridie Aldridge (10)
Thomas Reade Primary School

RAIN

I can water the land when
the ground starts to crack

And the gaps start to fill
as I cry my damp tears

I can banish the sun
as my tears drop down

Or as the sun sleeps
I start slowly to leak

I swirl around watering the ground
I run down windows and run down doors

I can spit, pour and make things wet
When I am done, I go back up to the sun.

Lisa Wood (11)
Thomas Reade Primary School

FIRE

I can burn down houses and trees
And make you run to the door with keys.
I can burn down candles
Or make hot handles.
Leaves I can burn and paper I can eat;
I can take your toys or the smell of burnt meat.
When I am angry, I fight and rant
And when I am gone, I lie as smoke.

Nicola North (10)
Thomas Reade Primary School

CHARGE OF THE FLY BRIGADE

Half a wing, half a wing,
Half a wing onward,
Away from the smack of the swat,
Flew the flies in hundreds.
'Beware of the swat ahead,
Fly to the door instead!'
Away from the smack of the swat,
Flew the flies in hundreds.

'Beware of the swat ahead,
Or else you will be dead!'
And then there was a smack
And one less fly came back.
They all tried not to cry,
They tried to reason why,
They knew they might well die,
So, away from the smack of the swat,
Flew the flies in hundreds.

Swat to the right of them,
Swat to the left of them,
Swat in front of them,
How could they escape?
Each fly tired, oh so well!
So boldly they flew onward,
Away from the smack of the swat,
Into the mouth of hell,
Flew the flies in hundreds.

Flapped all their wings out there,
Flapped as they turned in air,
Flying from the swat so close,
Or else they'd be flat as toast!

Claire Liddiard & Sara Talman (11)
Thomas Reade Primary School

THE SEA BRIGADE!

Half a shoal, half a shoal,
Half a shoal onward,
All in the oceans of fate,
Swam the six hundred.
Swiftly the shark jaws sped,
Snapping like a mad thing,
Into the ocean of fate,
Swam the six hundred.

Flashes of silver light,
Reflecting on the water,
Not though the brave fish knew,
More sharks were coming!
Fishes must not look back,
In case the sharks are nearer,
Hold their breath and wish for best.
Into the ocean of fate,
Swam the six hundred.

Sharks to the right of them,
Sharks to the left of them,
Sharks in front of them,
Circling and circling.
Fishes start to worry,
Into the jaws of terror,
Into the mouth of doom,
Swam the six hundred.

Oh the wild swim they made,
All the sea wondered,
Honour the trip they made!
Honour the sea brigade!
Noble six hundred!

Amber Parrott & Hannah Joyce (11)
Thomas Reade Primary School

CHARGE OF THE HAMSTER BRIGADE

Half a rodent, half a rodent
Half a rodent onwards
Into the garden of horror
Scrambled the sixty hamsters
'Forward the hamster brigade
Charge for the wheels!' he said

'Forward the hamster brigade!'
Was there a rodent dismayed?
Not that the hamster knew,
Someone had blundered,
Theirs not to make reply, theirs not to reason why
Theirs but to do and die
Into the garden of horror
Scrambled the sixty hamsters

Jaws to the right of them
Jaws to the left of them
Jaws behind them
Scratched and gnawed
Crawled with claws and teeth
While jaws and hero fell
They that had fought so well
Back from the patio of war
Back from 'no rodents' land
All that was left of them, left of sixty hamsters

When can their glory fade?
Oh the wild charge they made
All the house wondered
Honour the charge they made, honour the hamster brigade
Noble sixty hamsters.

Robbie Hand (10)
Thomas Reade Primary School

THE WIND

When the wind is howling,
Between the buildings,
It is a wolf, desperately searching
For its lost cubs.

When the wind is whistling
Through the trees,
It is a snake hunting
For its food.

When the flickering flames
Come flying out of your fire,
It is a dragon fighting
Against a warrior.

When the blowing umbrellas
Turn inside out,
It is a mysterious ghost
Spooking people.

When it is making a
Cold draught in the house,
It is a polar bear
Daydreaming around the house.

When the breaking branches
Come off the trees,
It is a dinosaur,
Stamping through the trees.

Lucy Tyler (9)
Thomas Reade Primary School

THE WHITE SEA HORSE

Galloping, thrashing, wild and white
His eyes are like diamonds against the night
With his flailing hooves and fearless eyes
Day upon day he roars
Roaring a roar that echoes the cliffs
Crashing down upon the shores
Endlessly crashing upon the shores

And when the night wind howls
And the moon sits silver in the sky
He rears up tall into the black
Moonlight reflecting upon his back
His sleek mane is a ghost in the sky
His squeal pierces the air . . . fly!

And when the sea is calm and still
Lapping against the shore
He is silent, trotting along the tide
Not a single squeal, not a single roar
He paws the ground, flicks his tail
Settles down upon his knees
He closes his eyes, falls quiet
Not a single whisper across the seas.

Mimi Kellard (10)
Thomas Reade Primary School

THE WIND

When the wind is howling between the buildings
It is a wolf looking for its dead cub

When the wind is whispering through the trees
It is a snake slithering in the dewy grass

When the wind is making a draught
It is a colossal vulture flying by

When the wind is flickering flames
It is a lion in an irritable mood

When the wind is blowing umbrellas inside out
It is a ghost rushing through the street

When the wind is breaking branches off trees
It is a T-rex trampling through the forest.

Aaron Jane (10)
Thomas Reade Primary School

THE SEA

The sea is a galloping horse,
Triumphant and black,
He trots along the shallows all day,
With his flowing tail and streamline mane,
Hour upon hour he canters,
The sizzling sandy shores
And oats, oats, oats, oats,
The great stallion roars,
Kicking his long legs and hooves.

When the winter wind blows
And the moon glimmers in the blue night sky,
He leaps through the air so proud, so proud,
Jumping his way into the cliffs,
He screams and screams long and loud.

But on quiet days in May or June,
As he trots along the sandy dune,
To the open seas again so soon,
He hangs his head down low,
Waves around his hooves will flow,
So still, so still, so very slow.

Jonathan Mallion (10)
Thomas Reade Primary School

Charge Of The Dog Brigade

Half a pack, half a pack, half a pack charging,
All in the alley of doom, ran the doggy hundred,
'Forward the dog brigade, woof!'
'Charge for the bones' he said, into the alley of doom
Ran the doggy hundred.

Bones to the right of them, bones to the left of them,
Bones to the front of them,
Volley'd and shatter'd,
Storm'd at with bone and ball, boldly they ran and fast,
Into the bins of bashing, into the tunnel of screams,
Ran the doggy hundred.

Flash'd all their claws bare, flash'd as they jumped in air,
Clawing the attackers their,
Charging an army, while,
All the street wonder'd,
Plunged in the battery trash.

Tom Hodson & Sanjay Sharma (10)
Thomas Reade Primary School

Lightning

I can shock people in seconds
I can burn the ground with my might
I can split a tree in half with force
I can strike hard any moment
I can fizzle people with my strength
My power is strong in the night
Be warned, I will hit at any moment.

Nishant Khataniar (10)
Thomas Reade Primary School

THE SEA

The sea like a swarm of bees
The pebbles are like melted sauce

The wind is like a strong eagle
The cliffs are like tall, broken buildings

The sand is like pieces of glass
The rocks are like sharp needles.

Andrew Eccles (10)
Thomas Reade Primary School

SURFING THE WAVES

Surfing the waves is fun
Under you go
Rough waves emerge
Flipping your board
Interesting dances on top
Nothing is better than surfing
Gigantic waves approach

The tide comes in and pushes you to shore
Heavy wind blows sand in your eyes
Everyone is surfing

Wetsuits cling to your body
Amazing action
Valuable boards are used
Everyone is in safe hands
Surfing the waves is fun!

Charlotte Whitlam (10) & Kayleigh Estus (11)
Tower Hill Primary School

NIGHT

The night mother is shy by day and everywhere by night,
She is comforting and speaks gently like the stars,
Quietly and caringly the cradle of night comforts a newborn baby,
While a grandad struggles to sleep
And returns to his grandson's bed
He snuggles down and slowly but surely falls into a deep sleep
Cradled by the night mother

Her face is as sweet as a rose
While her clothes are ripped and ragged
Her unwashed body has a distinctive smell

You will find her everywhere you look
She gives you good dreams
And takes away pain and nightmares
As she walks around, she is blinding
She can make you see nothing but black, pitch-black
Her jet-black hair waves in the wind
But as the sun dawns on Earth
She returns to the shadows shading her eyes
The night mother is shy by day and everywhere by night
She is comforting and speaks gently like the stars.

Luke Fry (11)
Tower Hill Primary School

FAVOURITE THINGS

I'm going to try to guess
All your favourite things,
It could be jewellery
Or a teddy bear that sings.
It could be your PlayStation,
With all the fancy games
Or maybe a doll,
That remembers all your names.

Perhaps you like sweeties best
Or chocolate Easter eggs,
Maybe it's your newest phone,
For mums, some washing pegs.
It could be a television
Or football instead,
Perhaps it's reading lots of books
Or like me, just going to bed.

Bethany Walker (10)
Witney Community Primary School

CHRISTMASTIME

You can hear the screams,
The laughter and carols.
Corks popping, paper noises are
Lovely sounds to hear.
The delicious smell of the turkey cooking,
The Christmas pudding.
On the side - oh it makes my mouth water!
Tasting the champagne with the fizz
Going up my nose,
Excited children stealing the raisins
From the fruity cake,
While adults aren't looking!
Feeling the bristly branches on the tree,
Surprise presents underneath.
The tinsel pricking your finger and sparkling
With the flashing lights as you pass by,
Outside the crunch of the newly-fallen snow,
As we build the snowman.
We ride on the sleigh with squeals of delight,
Enjoying our Christmas Day!

Charlotte Hewson (10)
Witney Community Primary School

WEATHER POEM

What is the moon?
The bike reflector of the universe.

Where does the rainbow end?
Inside the kindest leprechaun's heart.

Why does lightning only strike once?
Because it only has one good blast.

Who makes clouds?
God when he breathes.

When do the seasons change?
When all the gods get bored of the one they're in.

Where's the switch to turn off the sun?
In the man on the moon's house.

How does the rain fall?
The earth sucks it up when it's thirsty.

Who put the colours in the rainbow?
God's best friend with his set of permanent watercolour paints.

Steve Barney (10)
Witney Community Primary School

QUESTION AND ANSWER POEM

What is gold?
The hearts of the gods and the wisdom of the seas.

What are pearls?
Drops of mermaids' tears frozen by the winter's breeze.

What is silver?
The love and sorrow of all white doves.

What are sapphires?
Every happy dream that floats in the sky above.

What are diamonds?
Thousands of tiny wishes ready to be collected.

But the most precious treasure of all is love,
Which we are all blessed with.

Amber Lee (11)
Witney Community Primary School

TREASURE

When I saw him he was lovely,
He has soft, long hair with
Brown highlights.
He was all I wanted,
The best birthday present
Ever . . .

A dog!

He is very energetic
And when he runs
He looks like a greyhound.
When he chases the ball,
It's like watching wind.

When he is asleep,
It's like staring at
A cloud so soft and gentle
And when he's mine,
He's lovely.

Kirsty May Abberley (10)
Witney Community Primary School

SNOWDROPS

Snowdrops, such magical things,
Sparkling dreamily in the winter's sun,
In rows they glitter like an angel's wings,
Like precious crystals they shine,
Making the light scatter about,
Making shadows and patterns appear,
They light up the room like a glowing light bulb,
I love those little snowdrops,
They make my life complete,
But what makes me cry and weep,
Is when the little snowdrops
Fall down, down, down,
When the midwinter sun
Makes them drip,
Then they fall,
One by one,
Then they scatter like glass on the freshly-cleared path
And they've gone,
Never to be seen again.

Melissa Gray (11)
Witney Community Primary School

THE DOLPHINS

Beneath the pinky early morning sky
Calm, untouched by living creature,
The turquoise sea ripples in the gentle breeze
Catching the sun's warm rays of light
Making it glint and glitter like a jewel.

Suddenly, leaping high into the air
A gleaming, glistening dolphin;
Another and another, chasing, diving,
Jumping up higher and higher
Spraying droplets into the golden sun.

With a final flick of their mighty tails
As if from a silent signal,
They vanished into the mysterious depths
Abruptly as they had appeared,
Leaving the surface undisturbed, serene.

Sarah Dimond (10)
Witney Community Primary School

THE SCHOOL BELL RINGS

At 9:00 the school bell rings,
Another day again begins.
Our names are called out loud to see,
How many children today there will be.
We line up quietly to wait for the call,
To go down for assembly in the hall.
We sing, we listen, there are things people show,
But soon it's back to the classroom we go.
Our lessons this morning are literacy,
Followed by science and numeracy.
At 12:00 the school bell rings,
Now lunchtime and play begins.
We play for a while then in for lunch,
All you can hear is munch, munch, munch.
Back outside, hooray it's dry!
We all skip and run and jump so high.
At 1:00 the school bell rings,
The afternoon session now begins.
The teacher says it's boring history,
Oh! We thought it was geography!
The last lesson we have is music today,
What a noise we make when we play.
At 3:00 the school bell rings,
Great, now all the *homework* begins!

Charlotte Rowe (10)
Witney Community Primary School

GANG SHOW

March is coming, *yippee!* Here we go,
Look out Apollo, here comes the Gang Show!
Posters are plastered all over the walls,
George, Chippy, Mo are sending out photo calls.
The gang goes on, the band begins to play,
The curtain goes up, but we're in the way!
The rest of the gang will then start to sing,
While the dancers and I wait in the wing.
The music stops, the curtains fall,
Mo comes round with our last call.
The spotlights on, our turn has come,
I do love dancing, *hey* there's my mum!
We twist and spin, jump and jive,
Soon it's time for the next act to arrive.
I love the show, it comes once a year,
There's plenty of variety, have no fear.
Singing, dancing, acting too,
Everyone's coming . . . why don't you?

Cheryl Birdseye (11)
Witney Community Primary School

HOPE

Hope lies within the heart,
It is there to keep you company,
On your voyages and lifetime adventures,
It will do the same to you as it does to me.

It is there when you're feeling low,
It's there when you're high,
Hope is everywhere within you,
It's even in your thigh!

It's there with you from the beginning
And there until the end,
You'll never find anyone better,
With what love and hope it sends.

Shaun Killingbeck (10)
Witney Community Primary School

THE BURGLAR

When dark is out and lights are dim,
The only thing I see is him.
He's small and fat wearing, shiny black clothes,
He's also so ugly with that crooked nose.

He sneaks around the houses and streets,
Looking inside for some golden treats.
He finds a house and looks for a key,
Then bangs the door open, so suddenly.

When he's inside he looks around,
For creaky floorboards on the ground.
Then as quick as lightning he has seen,
A handbag on the table where no one's been.

When he hears a floorboard creak,
That's when he opens the bag and has a peek.
He's never been caught doing this before,
So he runs and hides and tries to ignore.

He ignores the yelling from the crowd
And tries to feel really proud.
But he can't, not this time,
So he gives himself in for this dirty crime.

Rebecca Jupp (10)
Witney Community Primary School

CAPTAIN SPRATT

Sat in my chair in the middle of the night,
I glimpsed a figure that gave me a fright,
Was it a bird? Was it a plane?
Or was it the ghost from Maple Lane?

He's haunted round here for many a year,
But really I know there's nothing to fear.
Dragging his ball and chain along,
Singing his jolly sailor's song.

Goes by the name of Captain Spratt,
A man of many words and goolish chat!
A man who lived a gallant life,
He bullied his children, but loved his wife.

He swifts into my room with his tales of the sea,
But he never ever frightens me,
Eaten by a whale and stung by a skate,
Captain Spratt's my very best mate.

Calum Hazell (10)
Witney Community Primary School

A WINTER'S NIGHT

As dusk falls, night creeps in,
Another cold and misty night is beginning.
Jack Frost will soon be here,
Making all the gardens sparkle.

Stars shine brightly in the clear night sky,
Surrounding the full silvery moon.
Owls are hooting in the trees,
Getting ready for their nights hunting.

Families keep warm indoors,
Getting ready to sleep till morning.
While all the night-time animals
Are waking, ready to start their day.

Laura Dowsett (11)
Witney Community Primary School

A FLICKER IN MY HEART

Deep in the heart a hope does dwell,
Beneath all that love and sorrow,
A little flicker in the depths,
In those cavernous empty spaces,
Lies the inner peace.

On the face,
That place of happy and sad,
The expressions show it all
And when the face grows long and sad,
The flicker of peace does fall.

In the eyes a tear does dwell,
When the sorrows live
And when that dwelling is too much,
The inner peace does give.

The heart does bulge if love comes near,
The outer peace invades
Throughout the time your love is here,
The inner peace does cave.

If you can keep your inner peace
Away from your desire,
If you can keep from cruel harm's way,
Your peace will rise up higher!

George Bone (10)
Witney Community Primary School

WHAT, HOW, WHEN POEM

What do you see
About you and me?
The stars in the sky
And deep in the sea

How do you choose where to go
If it's very dark
And covered with snow?

When do you choose
When to die?
When to help?
When to leave?
Whatever you do, choose or see.
Choose best for you and me.

Laura Hockey (11)
Witney Community Primary School

TREASURE

Treasure, treasure buried deep,
If I find it, I will keep
Digging here, digging there,
I can't find it anywhere.
Jewels and gems I must find,
But I am running out of time,
Diamonds, pearls and golden rings,
These are all precious things,
The time has come for me to go
But I will return tomorrow.

Amy Skidmore (10)
Witney Community Primary School

BLUE PLANET

The gentle surface of the sea,
Sparkles in the sunshine,
While the waves wash the sandy shores.

The bright cloudless sky,
Reflects beautifully above the turquoise sea.
The salty smell,
Makes me feel calm and relaxed.

The spray from the sea,
Made the air feel moist.

Beneath the surface of the sea,
The seaweed entwines the coral.
The many secrets of the sea
Are yet to be told.

Laura Grant (10)
Witney Community Primary School

THE PATH OF LIFE

Don't let jealousy block your way,
Let peace be with you every day.

Don't let hate grow in your mind,
Fate is something you must find.

Nightmares are nasty, they feed your fear,
Hope will catch your little tear.

Let humour tickle you with joy,
Don't let anger constantly annoy.

Only when death approaches,
You will drown in a host of memories.

Christopher James Barker (10)
Witney Community Primary School

It Was The Day

It was the day,
The day we met,
That I got,
My clever pet.

It was the day,
The day I broke my nose,
My clever pet,
Ate Mother's hose!

It was the day,
The day I came,
My pet ate,
My favourite game!

It was the day,
The day I got sick,
I threw my dog,
A great big stick.

It was the day,
The day my dad went to work,
My clever pet,
Ate my homework!

It was the day,
The day is snowed,
My clever pet,
Got a really bad cold.

It was the day,
The day we split,
I sadly dug,
My dog a pit.

Ashley Ramsey (11)
Witney Community Primary School

CLOUDS

Far above the ground,
Highest you can go,
Float white fluffy clouds,
Giant balls of feathers,
Big, peaceful monsters of the sky,
Gentle breezes carry them forwards,
As the birds glide swiftly below them.

Clouds are giant balls of candyfloss,
Shimmering in the air,
Engulfing anything in their path,
With a foamy mist of watery air.

Above the clouds is a fantastic sight,
A never-ending bed of soft, white cotton wool,
With the sun glittering on the surface of the clouds,
For miles and miles you can see,
It stretches out for infinity.

James Parry (10)
Witney Community Primary School

CHRISTMASES MISSED

I stand here looking at the Christmas tree,
Thinking of you in your far distant country,
Of all the Christmases you've missed
And still have to miss.
I think of the difference it would be to you
To just have one present.
I think of all the days you suffered,
Battling on regardless
And that is why I'm sending you pictures
Of Christmases passed here . . .

Emma Craig (11)
Woodcote CP School

I Wish I Had A Rocket

I wish I had a rocket to fly up into space,
But then I realised I was in a different place.
I would like to fly to Mars,
For then I would touch the stars.
As the moon shines bright,
Throughout the night,
I thought I saw a spaceship's headlight.
The aliens came to say hello,
I wasn't scared even though they had three heads
And greenish eyes and big round feet
Like apple pies.

George Blower (9)
Woodcote CP School

I Am A Little Bunny Rabbit

I am a little bunny rabbit
And I live in my hutch
I like being a bunny rabbit
And thank you very much.

Gemma Ford (8)
Woodcote CP School

My Anger

My anger is as red as molten lava,
My anger tastes like mouldy butter
My anger looks like a jellyfish
My anger sounds like a dolphin crying
My anger feels like a rotting cabbage.

Matthew Ploszynski (8)
Woodcote CP School

MY ANGER

My anger is the colour of boiling lava,
My anger tastes like rotten squid,
My anger smells like old eggs
My anger looks like jellyfish
My anger sounds like waves crashing on the rocks
My anger feels like a slug.

Leo Anderson (8)
Woodcote CP School

HAPPINESS

It is as silver as people having fun,
It smells like no more war-time anywhere,
It looks like everyone on holiday,
It tastes like chips and pizza,
It sounds like people being happy,
It feels like everyone playing with each other.

Connor Mattimore (8)
Woodcote CP School

IF I WERE...

If I were John and John were me,
He'll be six and I'll be three,
Then he'd be me and I'll be him.
If John were me and I were John,
He will be a girl and I'll be a boy
And I wouldn't have these trousers on.

Natasha Hyde (10)
Woodcote CP School

THE SEASIDE

Glasses, towels and books to read,
Sand, shells and of course seaweed.

Splashing of waves against the rocks,
Waters swaying to the metal padlocks.

A sunken ship, a treasure chest,
Scattered money east to west.

Children playing with buckets and spades,
Famous people having a sunbathe.

Rock pools everywhere,
Catching crabs from under there.

Children play piggy in the middle,
Others sing 'Hey Diddle Diddle.'

Land ahoy! The pirates would say,
Beautiful island, a wonderful day.

Genevieve Simpson (8)
Woodcote CP School

A WALK IN THE WINTRY WOODS

Look up at the bare trees
Look down at the frosty leaves
Green, red, yellow, brown, orange
Walking on the muddy leaves

Birds flying everywhere
Squirrels jumping from tree to tree
Rabbits jumping on the frosty leaves
Foxes hunting for their tea
Deer munching at the leaves.

Jade Marshall (9)
Woodcote CP School

BULLIED

Her face is streaked from crying,
She looks down at the ground.
You rarely see her smiling,
It's as though it's not allowed.

Her face is hidden in her book,
All the way through class.
She's scared that if she dares to look,
The bully will just laugh.

He teases and insults her
And calls her nasty names.
She's too afraid to tell anyone,
Afraid she will be blamed.

Do you know someone just like this?
Are they in the same school as you?
If so, then try to help them
Or you're just a big bully too!

Anje Wessels (10)
Woodcote CP School